# DITCH
# the
# GUESSWORK

Creating Reliable ROI for
Time-Starved Investors

**Steve Juetten, CFP®**

*To my
good friend
Jeff.
Kairwaysé,
Greeass!*

*Stee Jaatt*

Norsemen Books

## Disclaimers

# Praise for "Ditch the Guesswork"

*"Ditch the Guesswork" is a delightful and educational story of one couple's quest for financial understanding and empowerment. If you've ever wondered what it would be like to engage with a holistic financial advisor, read this book! I felt like I was there – listening to the discussions with Donna and Paul and their advisor. Each chapter focuses on key points all investors need to know. Steve Juetten, CFP® professional explains complex and at times controversial subjects simply and brilliantly."*

~ Sheryl Garrett, CFP, AIF
Founder, Garrett Planning Network, Inc.

*Steve Juetten's "Ditch The Guesswork" is wittily written in a conversational tone that provides timeless wisdom to investors of all levels. It is hard to argue with the straightforward logic presented in his book. It's a must read for anyone searching for clarity in the creation of their own financial plan.*

~ Bill Schultheis, Soundmark Wealth Management,
Author of "The Coffeehouse Investor"

*I make this book available to my tax clients because I know the positive impact it can have on their lives and financial well-being. Steve makes investing understandable for those who are not financially inclined. His advice holds true to long standing principles that work time and time again.*

~ Chris Davies, CPA, CMA

*I've followed Steve's investment advice for many years and have been delighted with how easy it is to consistently apply a few basic principles. Steve offers these same ideas in "Ditch the Guesswork" so anyone can follow them. Read this book and stop guessing about your investments and start making informed decisions.*

~ SHIRIN BHAN, PRESIDENT AND FOUNDER, KNB COMMUNICATIONS

*I love this book. Clear, concise, entertaining, easy to read with practical, actionable information for every investor no matter their stage of life. I wish I had met Steve earlier in my career.*

~ CYNTHIA GEDDES, MD

*Steve Juetten has been the financial advisor for my family for several years. His ability to navigate through all the complexities of the financial industry and clearly and simply communicate a plan tailored to my family's needs is remarkable. These clear, mature, intelligent qualities which I value so much in Steve also shine through in his new book. I highly recommended it!*

~ GREGORY SUMMERS, MD

*I have been working with Steve for many years. "Ditch the Guesswork" and his philosophy take all the noise out of investing and have allowed me to focus on what is truly important. I wish I had read this book in my early 20s. Definitely a book that I will give to my kids.*

~ SUNDEEP BHAN, CEO OF MEDIVO, INC.

*I love the* "Ditch the Guesswork" *book. Steve Juetten has been my wife's and my personal financial advisor for several years. Steve's book is a must read for a busy person who wants to invest in a way that's simple and easy to follow, and easy to match to his or her personal financial situation and preferences.*

~ Peter Raulerson, Partner, The Paramarketing Group, LLC

*Having a Wharton MBA and ten years of Wall Street equity research experience, I'm pleased to see that Steve's book takes complex subjects and makes them understandable to almost any reader. Share it with anyone who asks how to approach investing.*

~ Ben Rooks, Founder and Principal, ST Advisors, Inc.

*Wall Street hasn't always made it easy for many of us to fully understand what is going on in the markets and especially in how we should navigate this complex and foggy world. The conversation inside* "Ditch the Guesswork" *is not only simple in its approach, but is also exactly what we all deserve to hear from our trusted advisors. I have known Steve for years both professionally and personally. Who you see with Steve is who you get. Straightforward, compassionate, empathic, competent, and honest. He tells you what you need to hear—not just what the media sells us or we don't want to hear. Enjoy the journey he takes you on in* "Ditch the Guesswork." *Follow his advice or reach out to work with him as your trusted advisor.*

~ John Schmick, trusted friend and colleague
with over 30 years of institutional investment
management consulting experience with
many of the industry's marquee firms

# Contents

# Acknowledgments

I could not have written this book without exceptional help and support. Accordingly, thanks to Amy Shappell, CFP® who provided the peer review for the content and prevented me from blundering too badly (I still own any and all mistakes in the text; Amy can only do so much!); Sue Juetten, who edited the first draft of the manuscript and helped boil this down to its pure essence (thanks big sister); Chris Flett, my coach and mentor; Dan Maul, my friend, trusted adviser and fishing buddy; Bill Baren and Patrick Dominguez for their inspiration and guidance; Carrie Mosley, our company operations manager, who makes our business run smoothly so I can do the work I love to do; Victoria Vinton, who created the book cover and made the illustrations and text look good and made sure it was readable; Jennifer Parrett, who took the rough manuscript and made it a workable document.

I also want to thank all the clients I've been privileged to work with during my career. I have learned from each of you and am grateful that you have allowed me to serve you. Donna and Paul are the embodiment of you all.

And to Nancy, my wife, I give my deepest gratitude and appreciation. You are the light of my life and the wind beneath my wings. You are the best. I also want to thank our son Kyle for coming into our lives. I became a financial advisor so I could be around while you grew up into the exceptional young man you are becoming.

Finally, I stand on the shoulders of the greats in my field and I am grateful. I have been inspired by John Bogle, Harry Markowitz, William Sharpe, John Ellis, William Bernstein, Daniel Solin and Larry Swedroe. I extend a very special thanks to Bill Schultheis, the Coffeehouse Investor, for his inspiration, thought, leadership and support.

# Introduction
## *Why another book about investing?*

There are lots of books about investing out there. At last count, on Amazon.com there are approximately 114,547 books on investing. More get added every month. If you read a book a day, it would take you over 313 years to get through every one of them (but I assume you want to retire someday!) Why does the world need another book on investing? Because in today's 24-7 news cycle, and an instant information overload world, you have too much data and not enough information to make good investment decisions. As a result, you guess about the best way to take care of your investments. You guess about which adviser to use. You guess about how to invest your money. The managers of the mutual funds you use guess about how to pick stocks or bonds. There's entirely too much guessing going on and not enough people making informed choices.

Instead of following a plan that provides a reliable return on your investment (ROI), you're left with more questions than answers. You're left wondering what works? Why does my portfolio never seem to grow as much I hope it will? What can I expect to happen with my portfolio when the investment markets go up or down? Whom should I trust to give me advice? In other words, you engage in "Guesswork Investing."

What if I offered you an investment approach that takes the guesswork out of investing and instead offers five benefits?

1. Simple
2. Effective
3. Efficient
4. Sustainable
5. Flexible

Would that appeal to you? I think it probably does. That's why I wrote "Ditch the Guesswork: Creating Reliable ROI for the Time-Starved Investor." I recommend that you follow an approach called Strategic Asset Class Investing (ACI for short). This is not a new idea, nor is it solely mine. For more than 60 years, ACI has given informed investors a way to invest that has been successful.

The idea for this book came to me while I was outlining an article for my blog (www.finpath.com) on common investing mistakes I see regular investors make. When the list reached 52 items, I realized what the world does not need is another investment book; what the world needs is an approach that helps investors avoid those 52 mistakes created mostly by guessing what might work. You need an approach that helps you be a successful investor and provides reliable returns on your investment. You need to understand the features – and especially – the benefits of Strategic Asset Class Investing.

I won't lie to you. The future is unknowable and therefore making investment choices involves uncertainty. But if you follow the approach I outline here, asset class investing, you will take most of the guesswork out of investing. You will still have uncertainty, but you'll have a solid, time-tested investment method that has worked for the last 60 years.

I am a CERTIFIED FINANCIAL PLANNER™ professional, which means I've studied the whole realm of personal finance. In my company, we work with clients across the full spectrum of personal finance topics: goal setting, wise use of cash flow and debt, personal insurance, planning for college, retirement planning, efficient tax strategies and estate planning. Investing is just ONE aspect of personal finance that we help our clients address and it's not even the most important one for many clients. It's just one aspect and something you need to get right for financial security.

## Who This Book is For

I wrote this book for anyone who wants reliable Return on their Investment (ROI) and:

- Wants to spend their free time doing something other than investing, like enjoying fun activities with their family, doing hobbies and focusing on their career;

- Thinks of investing as a means to an end NOT a zero sum game,

- Is confused and befuddled by all the noise coming from Wall Street, and

- Wants a way to invest that is effective and efficient, time-tested, based on academic research and, yet, easy to understand.

In short, this book is for anyone who wants reliable ROI from their investments and to do it in an effective and efficient way. That's the promise of Strategic Asset Class Investing.

In this book, you will learn how to invest using asset classes and thereby how you can do better than 85% of professionals in a typical year (aka "the smart money"). And based on an unscientific sampling, in my experience, it works better than the way 99.9% of your neighbors, family and people you work with follow.

## Who This Book Is Not For

If you want a get rich quick book, this is not for you.

- If you want to "beat the market" so you can brag to your friends, this is not for you.

- If a large part of your self-worth is tied up in your net worth, this is not for you.

- If you want to spend loads of time pouring over charts and newsletters to pick the "next Apple," this is not for you.

If you think of investing as a game, don't waste your time reading this book. Go to a casino or play racquetball. Here's a little secret a typical financial adviser won't tell you: successful investing should be satisfying, profitable and bring peace of mind. It will not be exciting, entertaining or exhilarating.

# PART 1

# WHAT, WHY
# AND HOW COME?

# What's An Asset Class?

I was sitting in my office late one Thursday and the phone rang. "Hello, this is Steve Juetten, how can I help you."

"My name is Paul Moore and I've been looking at your website and would like to talk about how your investing approach might be able to help my wife and me."

"Hi Paul and thanks for calling. Do you have a couple of minutes right now to tell me a little about your situation and I can answer some questions if you'd like?"

"Yes, I have time now. My wife Donna and I are in our early 50's and are frustrated by our investing experience. We've tried investing on our own and that didn't work out so well. Neither of us has much time or, frankly, much interest in investing. Our kids are grown and we both have busy jobs and we like to hike, and boat and be outside enjoying hobbies. Then we tried an investment adviser that my brother uses and that didn't work out either. I felt like he was talking around me all the time and I never could get a straight answer from him about what he was doing and what it was costing us. So we're out of guesses about what to do."

"Thanks Paul. I hear this story a quite a bit so you're not alone. It is frustrating to be an investor and not know what to do or who to trust, isn't it?"

"It sure is! So I see on your website that you follow something called 'Strategic Asset Class Investing.' What the heck is an asset class?"

"An asset class is nothing more than a type of investment that acts differently than any other kind of investment."

"You mean like stocks, bonds and mutual funds, right?"

"Stocks and bonds are different asset classes, but a mutual fund is a basket that holds either one type of asset, like stocks, or some mutual funds hold several asset classes. Other asset classes include the stocks from developed countries outside the U.S., bonds from other countries, real estate, cash, and even commodities, rental property and commercial real estate."

"Wow. You mean we have to own commodities and rental property and investments like that?"

"Not at all. Those are just some types of asset classes. In fact most people only hold five or six asset classes in their portfolios. Some items you might own are **not** asset classes. For example, your house, personal items like jewelry or collectibles like stamps and coins."

"Okay. I get it now. An asset class is just a kind of investment but not like a car or a house, right? But what makes something an asset class?"

"Do you remember that I said earlier that an asset class acts differently than any other kind of investment? That's the key to asset class investing. An investor needs to own assets that act differently at different times. The fancy word for this is 'non-correlation', meaning acting independently from each other. An investor needs to own assets that are different than one another because not all assets go up or down at the same time. There are times, like in 2008, when most assets acted alike, but not all. For example, did you know that U.S. bonds were a safe haven for many investors in 2008? In fact, the Vanguard Intermediate Term Bond Index went up almost 5% that year."

Paul answered, "I didn't know that. It sure seemed like all our investments went down a lot then. So using different asset classes is a way to make sure you don't lose money?"

"I wish that were true," I said. "No, using asset classes is a way to *balance* risk and return, but I'm afraid nothing always goes up. Asset class investing makes sure that an investor's portfolio is diversified across a broad spectrum of investments. Our clients use the asset classes they choose and diversify within those asset classes. For example, if an investor wants to own stocks, we may suggest that they own U.S. and non U.S. stocks and if they own bonds, we may suggest they own U.S. and non U.S. bonds."

"Okay, that makes sense. What about my insurance policies? My insurance guy is all over me telling me I should 'invest' in more insurance and buy annuities. Donna and I are suspicious. What do you think?"

I answered, "For most people, life insurance is **not** an investment; it's for protecting you against a large loss. There are some circumstances where life insurance may be an investment, but from what you've shared so far, not for you and Donna. Annuities can be an investment, but we're very cautious about them too because of the high cost and the fact that money is locked in and you can't get it out without penalties for a long time. Investors need to be very careful around insurance products."

Paul was silent for a moment and I could tell he was thinking about his next question.

"Okay Steve, I'm going to make an executive decision even though Donna is not here right now. We'd like to meet you and continue the conversation. How do we do that?"

"Thanks Paul. I would like to meet the two of you too. I'll have my assistant send you my calendar for the rest of the month and you and Donna can pick a time to come in and see me. She'll send you a couple of documents to complete and bring with you too. One is a goals worksheet so I can get an idea of what you and Donna see for yourselves in the next five years and the other is a personal balance sheet. It's pretty simple, but it gives us a common document to use when we talk. Of course, there is no cost for this get acquainted session. How does that sound?"

"That sounds fine. I know Donna will be excited to move ahead on our investments too. She knows more about this than I do and is unhappy with the way we've been doing this for a long time. I look forward to meeting, and thanks. By the way, don't you want me to bring in our investment statements?"

"Not really. This will be more of a get acquainted session and I'm not too concerned with what you have in your investment accounts now. Remember, our investment approach is different than what you have now so rather than look backward, I'd rather start to look forward. See you in a week or so. Thanks again for calling."

Paul sounded upbeat when he replied, "Okay, sounds good."

After we hung up, I wondered how Paul and Donna would behave as a couple. I'd just talked to Paul privately and couples sometimes are very different when they're together and talking about money compared to when they're alone. I was reminded of the few times that I was in a room with a couple that didn't get along. The tension made me uncomfortable and we usually don't take couples like that as clients. I hoped that Donna and Paul would be enjoyable to be around. I liked Paul and wanted to help them if I could.

I turned back to my computer and continued reading an email from a client who is in Germany on a once in a lifetime family trip. Donna and Paul will have their chance to live their dreams soon enough, I mused.

## Key Points

- An asset class is nothing more than a type of investment that acts differently than any other kind of investment. Some asset classes are not needed or not available cost effectively. Examples of assets that might be in a portfolio:
  - » U.S. and non-U.S. stocks
  - » U.S. and non-U.S. bonds
  - » Real Estate, Investment Trusts (REITs)
  - » Cash
  - » Alternative investments: commodities, stock of private companies, rental residential real estate, commercial real estate
- Financial items that are **not** asset classes:
  - » Your house
  - » Collectibles like stamps and art
  - » Cash for emergencies

- » Wine
- » Jewelry
- Insurance is not normally an asset class.
  - » Good for transferring risk of a large loss to someone else
  - » Annuities can be an asset class, but have high costs and are complicated
  - » Be cautious around insurance products; most are **sold** by good salespeople and few are **purchased** by educated investors.

**Notes:**

# Why Asset Class Matters

A few weeks later, Paul and Donna came into our company conference room and we introduced ourselves. In our opening chit chat, I was pleased to see that Paul and Donna seemed to be at ease with each other. We talked about where they were from originally, their kids and what they do for a living. But I could see that Paul was anxious to get started. He started talking and pushed a folder towards me.

"We prepared the documents you asked for. The goals worksheet was a good exercise for us. We hadn't thought about what we wanted to do for the next five years in a long time. The balance sheet was pretty easy to do because most of that information is online. "

Donna interrupted Paul. "Before we get into that, Paul told me about your phone conversation and I had a few questions first. Is that okay?"

Encouraged by her interest, I replied, "Of course. This is the time to put all questions on the table. This is a get acquainted session for us all. I have an agenda in mind, but it's meant to be loose and lets us follow whatever path makes the most sense. Fire away."

Donna leaned forward. "Thank you. Paul tells me you believe in using different asset classes to invest and I know what that means, but my question is *why does that matter?*"

I looked at Paul and he was nodding. "That's an excellent question Donna", I replied. "I think you would agree that every investor wants to balance risk and return, right?" Both nodded. "So we use an approach called ***strategic asset class investing*** (ACI for short) because it's the most reliable, efficient, time-tested and academically proven way to balance risk and return. Here, look at this diagram."

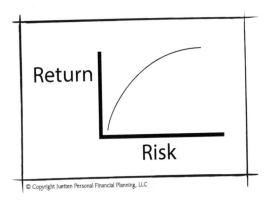

"Across the bottom is risk, we'll define that in a minute. Up the side is return. A guy by the name of Harry Markowitz was able to prove that all investments fall along this line. He won the Nobel Prize for creating this graph. Now everyone, me, you, my aunt Tilda, wants to invest up here." I put a big star in the upper left of the graph.

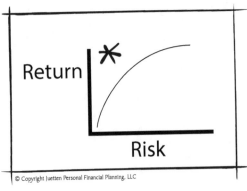

"But there's no such thing as a free lunch when it comes to investing. Markowitz proved that this whole area above the line is not available to us. All investments fall along this path. And our job as investors is to invest our money as close to this line as possible. **Our goal as an investor is to get as much return as we can for the amount of risk we're willing to take. That's why asset class investing matters. It gives the investor a way to balance risk and return in an understandable, proven way.** Does that make sense?"

Both Donna and Paul nodded thoughtfully; then Donna put another question to me. "What do you mean by risk? You said we'd define that term. Is that the crazy ups and downs in the Dow and S&P 500 we see on Cramer?"

"Well, first, Cramer is an entertainer and I hope to persuade you not to pay attention to him and his fellow talking heads. It's entertaining, but not helpful to you. So let's talk about this thing called 'risk' I mentioned.

"We define risk in two ways: First, there are the crazy ups and downs in markets that you mentioned. For the most part, that kind of risk is short term and we define this kind of risk as volatility. The second kind of risk is the failure to reach your long term goals. Here is a key point to keep in mind: avoiding one kind of risk exposes you to the other. This is important. There is no way to avoid both kinds of risk."

Paul sat back and said, "I never thought about investment risk that way. Can you give me an example?"

"Sure, the best way to avoid the short term ups and downs is to hold only cash in your accounts." I wrote in the word "cash" on the diagram.

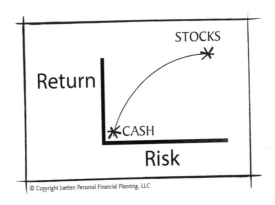

Paul interrupted, "But cash earns almost nothing!"

"You're right, but that's the way to avoid volatility, right?" Paul nodded as I continued. "But the problem is that because cash earns almost nothing you probably won't reach your long-term goals." I pointed to the word "stocks" on the other end of the curved line. "Historically, stocks have earned the most return, but with the highest volatility."

Now Donna chimed in. "Okay that makes sense. If we want to avoid stock market ups and downs, we have to accept very low returns. But if we want to make a large return, we have to accept more short-term ups and downs. And that's where asset allocation comes in, right?"

I continued. "Yes, that's where asset allocation comes in. But keep in mind that asset allocation is no guarantee that you won't have some ups and downs or that you're guaranteed to reach your long-term goals. Investing involves taking on risk. That's why some people sit on cash. They are so afraid of any risk that they just stand still."

Paul and Donna looked a little disappointed. Like most investors, they seemed to want a guarantee of success and investing doesn't work like that. I pushed on.

"Here is something maybe you didn't know. Let's say you have two portfolios, A and B. They hold different assets and different amounts of each asset. Most investors don't realize that **over 90% of the variation in returns of these two portfolios comes from the difference between how the two portfolios divide their money among asset classes.** The other 10% comes from a variety of factors including what individual securities they hold."

Paul interjected. "Wait a minute. I thought the big difference is due to stock picking and market timing. When to get in and out of the markets and how to find the next Apple or Google stock. That's not true?"

"Nope. All the talking heads who claim to be experts, your current investment adviser and probably your neighbor are focusing on the wrong thing. They're thinking about the donut hole and not the donut."

Donna was silent and I could tell she was listening carefully. She said, "This is very good. So why do most people focus on the wrong aspect of investing?"

"I think most people get it wrong for several reasons. The two most important are that the future is unknowable and markets are efficient, but our human nature and many other challenges also get in the way. Let me explain and then I want to ask you a question.

"Most people invest by trying to guess the future, but that's impossible. Because knowing the future is impossible, most investors *guess* what might happen next. They go through all sorts of pseudo-scientific analysis and research to support their position about what will happen next. But it's doomed to fail, because no one knows what will happen next. And that's where human nature gets in the way.

"There are all sorts of biases and behaviors that we engage in that hurt our chances of investment success. For example, we live in a culture of instant gratification, and good investing requires patience. We want to keep up with the Joneses and brag about our investing prowess at the company party."

Donna nudged Paul and said, "Like your pal Charles, right?" Paul nodded ruefully.

I continued. "There are about 10 behavioral biases we have that get in our way. Asset class investing assumes that the future is unknowable and asset class investors don't play the 'guess what happens next' game. And asset class investing works to offset our human nature because it takes the guesswork out of investing and uses a sound, disciplined approach instead. If an investor is willing, asset class investing can change his or her behavior to create a reliable return on investments.

"And one more thing: **A critical key to investment success is consistency**. You have to keep doing what works over a long period of time in order to succeed. If an investor follows one approach until she is disappointed, then switches to another guru or investing approach, she can't succeed. Once an investor commits to asset class investing, it is sustainable. Remember: asset class investing has worked over a very long period of time."

Donna and Paul looked at each other and then me. Donna stood up and asked where the rest room was so she could take a break. As she left, she asked another good question, "I understand what asset class investing is and why it matters, but does it work?"

## Key Points

- **Strategic Asset Class Investing** combines different investment types (asset classes) into an investment portfolio.

- Investors' goal: balance risk and return

  » Asset class investing: most reliable, efficient, time-tested and independently proven approach.

- "Risk" has two meanings:

  » Short term ups and downs of investment markets (volatility)

  » Failure to reach goals

- 90% of the variation in portfolio returns is due to differences in how money is divided between asset classes, not which securities are used or when they are purchased.

  » Most investors get this wrong.

  » Human nature leads to decision errors like market timing, following the herd and panic selling; asset class investing makes human nature less of an obstacle.

## Notes:

# Does Asset Class Investing Work?

When Donna returned, I said to her and Paul, "As you left, you asked another good question we need to answer: does Strategic Asset Class Investing achieve its stated goals? Let me start by asking you both a question. What is one of your financial goals?"

Paul laughed and Donna smiled. Paul said, "You know the answer to that question, counselor, because it was the first goal we wrote down on the homework you asked us to prepare. You have it right there. We wrote something like 'our goal in the next 12 months is to create a reliable, understandable investment plan that will help us reach our long-term financial goals.' Right?"

I smiled back and said, "Yes, I knew the answer and I wanted to remind you both that you had listed that as a goal. So Donna, when you ask if asset class investing works, you mean is it reliable, understandable and will it help you reach your long-term goals, right?"

Donna added, "And now that we're talking about this, the investment approach can't take too much of our time. Paul and I are busy enough as it is and we want to do fun activities on the weekends and not spend them poring over our investment statements."

"I hear that" I replied, "You're busy and want to have time to follow the pursuits you love. If I may, this is what **I hear you're looking for: an investment approach that is simple to understand, effective and efficient**. Well, asset class investing has these benefits and some others we'll talk about in a few minutes, but let's talk about bottom line results now."

Pointing to the diagram I had drawn earlier, I continued, "Remember this risk and return diagram? What we want as investors is to be as close to this curved line as possible. We want to receive the most return for the amount of risk we're willing to take. The further out on the line you go, the more risk you take on. Risk here means both volatility and the probability of failing to reach your goals. Most portfolios we see are about here:

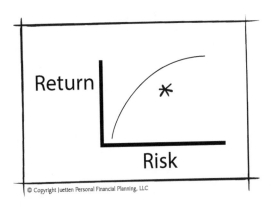

© Copyright Juetten Personal Financial Planning, LLC

"We call this an **in**efficient portfolio because the investor is taking on too much risk for the return she is getting. What we want as investors is to be here:

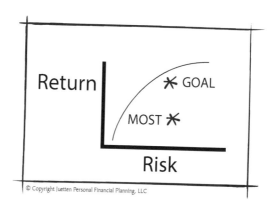

© Copyright Juetten Personal Financial Planning, LLC

"Note that the second X is not touching the line. Markowitz tells us that a portfolio on the line is a 'perfect' portfolio and that's not possible in the real world because there are some factors that reduce a portfolio's return."

Paul added, "Sort of like drag on an airplane. The better-designed airplanes have less drag and are more efficient. "I nodded. "Yes, that's right. For example, costs are a drag on the effectiveness of a portfolio. "

Donna chimed in, "Not to get us off track, but what are some other factors that drag on a portfolio's return?"

"Well, in any kind of portfolio the two biggest drags are high costs and human behavior. In a taxable portfolio, you can add the impact of taxes. The higher the cost of running a portfolio and the more mistakes we make managing a portfolio, the lower the returns. Or the higher the risk in some cases."

Donna replied, "I can see that. Paul and I have wondered about the costs that our investment adviser charges. We made him tell us how much we paid him last year because we couldn't find that number anywhere. He told us he charges us 1% of our portfolio value, but just the way he said it makes me wonder if we got the full story."

I nodded and said, "You may be right that your investment adviser might not have told you the full answer. We'll talk about costs and human behavior a little later." Donna nodded thoughtfully as I continued, "So one way to measure a portfolio's **effectiveness** is to determine how close to the line it is. There have been numerous academic studies that have looked at this issue and overwhelming evidence points to the fact that asset class investing is consistently the most effective way to invest money over a long period of time. Compared to most other methods of investing, ACI has the best net return for the amount of risk that an investor is willing to take on. In other words, Strategic Asset Class Investing has the best ROI.

Donna leaned forward and said one word, but with a smile, "Proof?"

I was beginning to like Donna and Paul very much. I said to them, "Trust but verify, right? Okay, don't take my word for it. Let me give you some information from three different studies that support asset class investing as a reliable way to generate ROI.

"The first study was done by a company called Dalbar.[1] They are an independent research group that studies the effectiveness of individual investor behavior. Every year they publish a report after analyzing investor behavior. Here are the findings from their latest report.[2]" I read to them:

- "In 2014, the average stock mutual fund investor *underperformed* the S&P 500 by a little more than 8%

---

1 www.dalbar.com
2 "Advisor Perspectives" April 8, 2015 (www.advisorperspectives.com)

- In 2014, the average fixed income mutual fund investor *underperformed* a widely used bond index by almost 5%.

- As of the end of 2014, the 20-year annualized S&P return was 9.85% while the 20-year annualized return for the average stock mutual fund investor was only about 5%, a gap of more than 4.5%.

- In 8 out of 12 months in 2014, investors guessed right about the market direction the following month. Despite 'guessing right' 67% of the time in 2014, the average mutual fund investor was not able to come close to beating the market based on the actual volume of buying and selling at the right time.

"And the number one reason that investors underperform is irrational behavior." I finished reading. "Dalbar defined nine irrational investment behaviors and noted that two cause the most problems:

- **Loss Aversion,** which leads to selling a security at the worst possible time – panic selling – or staying in cash for fear of moving into an investment, and

- **Herding**… following what everyone else is doing. Many times this leads to 'buy high/sell low' which is the opposite of what an investor wants to do."

Donna stopped me. "Do I understand you correctly that the average investor earned more than 4.5% *less* than the S&P 500 index over the last 20 years and 8% less in 2014? That makes me sick. That's probably what's been happening to us, Paul. No wonder we feel like we're not doing very well."

Paul chimed in, "I don't think we're guilty of panic selling, but we sure seem to follow the herd. Say, that's one thing I like about asset class investing. It seems like if we do that, we won't be following the herd, will we?"

I nodded and said, "You get the idea from the Dalbar study that the average investor doesn't do very well compared to a single index. A financial adviser I admire for the way he communicates with clients, Carl Richards, coined a term that describes the negative effect that behavior has on investment returns. He called it the 'behavior gap'[3] and created this simple illustration to make the point." I drew this picture on the pad in front of me.

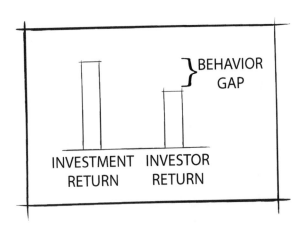

Paul and Donna looked at the illustration with interest. I continued, "For the second proof point, let's review the results of a study done of supposedly smart money managers at major pension funds." I pulled out another report:

"In a book that Charles Ellis[4] wrote, he cites a study of 100 major

---

3 "The Behavior Gap" by Carl Richards
4 "Winning the Loser's Game" by Charles D. Ellis

pension plans. Pension plans are run by very smart people who can afford to hire all the experts they want. In the study that Ellis cites,

"...not one of the pension plans had improved its rate of return as a result of its effort at market timing. This is a term we haven't discussed yet, but we will," I interjected. "In fact, 89 of the 100 pension plans lost as a result of 'timing' – and their losses averaged a daunting 4.5 percent over the five year period studied."

Paul shook his head and said, "Donna, you know your friend Beth is an engineer with the City. She has a pension plan. I always thought a pension plan was run by really smart people."

I added, "And just to add fuel to the fire, CALPERS, the California Public Employees Retirement Systems, last year stopped using hedge funds because they are too expensive and the results are not there. A hedge fund is a special type of investment company that is run by some of the supposedly smartest money people. Hedge funds are generally trying to time when to buy or sell securities.

"I have one more study to show you. Look at this chart based on an ongoing study done by the Standard & Poors Company[5]:

5  S&P Dow Jones Indices, McGraw Hill Financial

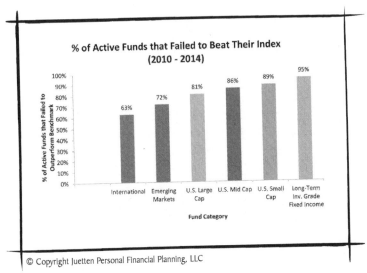

"This chart shows the percent of actively managed mutual funds that have not beaten their un-managed index over the last five years. 'Actively managed' means these are funds that use market timing to try to beat the market. As you can see, the vast majority of actively managed mutual funds have not been able to provide better returns. Strategic Asset Class Investing uses passive funds that try to earn the average return for an asset class."

Paul asked, "I sometimes get these ads for investment newsletters that proclaim how good they are at predicting the next market move. What do you think of those?"

"I have stats on those too." Here they are in this handout, "In a study done by a couple of guys named Graham and Campbell, they analyzed the advice given by 237 investment newsletters that covered over 15,000 market timing recommendations. They concluded that while some newsletters at certain times appeared to have made recommendations that worked out, it was no better than what could be expected from random recommendations. In other words, the investor would have done better following a solid asset allocation approach rather than following the market timing recommendations offered by these newsletters."

Paul interrupted and asked somewhat defensively, "You keep saying 'market timing.' Do you mean like day trading or something? We've never done that and our investment adviser says he doesn't do it either. So why are we talking about 'market timing' like it's what we do now?"

"Good question, Paul," I offered. "I use the term 'market timing' as a general term because that's what the majority of investment approaches that are not strategic asset allocation really are. Most investors, mutual funds and investment professionals are trying to pick a stock or market sector that they believe is undervalued and buy it before anyone else realizes it. That's market timing. Another way to think about it is this: if we believe the future is unknowable, the only way to pick a winning stock or mutual fund is to guess that it's going to go up before everyone else does. In other words, time the purchase before it goes up in value.

"It's the same thing with selling a security using anything other than strategic asset class investing. How do you think your investment adviser decides when it's time to sell a mutual fund?"

"Not sure."

"He or his firm or someone guesses that the fund has achieved its maximum value for the time being and sells it. In other words, they guess the timing is right to sell it. That's market timing."

I continued, "One problem with market timing is that a large percentage of the total gain that a stock or mutual fund earns occurs in a short period of time and we don't know in advance when that's going to happen. So a market timer has to own a stock or mutual fund when it's on an upward run or the market timer misses much of the gain.

"On the other side, if a market timer is going to avoid a down market, she has to guess that correctly too. As you've probably noticed, stocks don't go up or down in a uniform pattern. If they did, we could all be stock market geniuses. Trying to guess when a security is going to go up or down is nearly impossible over a reasonable period of time. If a market timer is wrong about when to buy a security, or when to sell that security, then she or he is going to be losing a lot of their or your money."

Paul perked up and added, "I was in the bookstore the other day and saw a headline in one of the personal finance magazines that said something like 'Four Stocks to Buy (and What to Sell) to Outperform the Market in 2016'. I never really thought about it, but that's market timing, isn't it?"

I nodded. "That's right, Paul. It's a subtle come-on to get you to buy the magazine. Here is one last statistic for you to chew on. A couple of researchers calculated that for market timing to pay, the person making the trades needs to be correct about 75% of the time. Other research suggests the number is even higher. That's being right at least three-quarters of the time about when to buy and sell. Almost impossible to do over a reasonable period of time. An asset class investor doesn't need to worry about that.

"Sometimes the media will make a big deal about some supposed expert market timer. I warn people not to confuse luck and skill." Donna cocked an eyebrow at me and said, "Not sure what you mean by that." I happily gave her an example. "Donna, suppose you put

100 people in a room and gave each of them a quarter and told them to flip the coin in the air. The ones that flipped 'heads' stay in the room and the ones that flipped 'tails' had to leave the room. After six rounds of coin flipping, you would likely have one person left in the room. Would you consider that person a coin flipper with superior skill or someone who was lucky?"

Donna answered, "Lucky, of course. I get your point."

Paul looked thoughtful and asked another question. "You just said one problem with market timing is that they have to be right about 75% of the time. Is another problem that it costs a lot to be buying and selling frequently?"

"You got it," I said. "All that buying and selling and the research that goes into trying to decide when to buy and sell is expensive. We can go into this more detail if you want, but in general, the average mutual fund expense ratio is about 1.2% and we can double that cost for trading. The average passively managed mutual fund expense ratio is about .3% and with trading costs you can add about .15% for a total cost of about .45%. The difference is about 2%. And the investor pays that expense. That doesn't include the fees an adviser collects either."

Paul looked pained, but said nothing.

Donna nodded and said, "Okay, I get it. Market timing is not the way to go." Paul nodded in agreement. Donna pulled the S&P chart closer to her and studied it for a minute, nodded again and said, "Okay, I'm convinced that asset class investing works better than any other approach. At least better than any of the ways to invest we've been doing. What else do we need to know on the question I asked that started all this."

I chuckled and said, "I know this is a lot of information and I hope I haven't overwhelmed you. Let me wrap up this long-winded answer with a couple of other points.

"First, keep in mind that the time period used to measure the effectiveness of an investment approach is important. You'll see many mutual funds claiming to be #1 in some area like big cap stocks or emerging markets. If you read the fine print of those ads, you'll often see odd time periods like from October 9 to August 11 or something like that. We call this 'data mining' and it's a sales tactic that mutual funds sometimes use. If I want to make my mutual fund look good, I find a few months when the approach worked well and use that to tout my fund's superior performance. So don't believe what you read without reading the fine print.

"Speaking of time periods, with asset class investing, there will always be periods of time when an asset class portfolio underperforms a benchmark like the S&P 500 or something like that. Because an asset class portfolio holds a basket of asset classes that act differently from one another, some of the asset classes will be down while others are up. The temptation is to sell the asset classes are doing poorly and load up on the ones that are doing well. We have to resist that urge."

Paul, the skeptical one of this couple, said, "Can you give me an example of that?"

"Sure. In 2014 and 2015, non-U.S. stocks did poorly compared to U.S. stocks. Commodities and natural resources also did poorly compared to U.S. stocks and even U.S. bonds. We had many clients that were nervous after the second year in a row of this difference and kept asking us if we thought that non U.S. stocks and commodities were worth holding. Our answer was always the same: you either rely on the research around asset class investing and believe in asset class investing or you don't. If you do, then we hold all the asset classes. It's worked over time and will likely keep doing so. We know it's hard not to want to get in there and start making tactical changes to a portfolio, but if a client does that, they are succumbing to one of the two deadly sins that we looked at in the Dalbar study. The sin of herding – doing what everyone else is doing.

"Here is something we tell all our clients. Want to know the real secret to successful investing? It's the three 'P's' followed consistently. The three P's are:

**Persistence** – sticking with an approach and not changing from one 'expert' to another;

**Perspective** – keeping a long-term view knowing that investment markets fluctuate and we must ignore the short term in order to get to our long-term goals;

**Patience** – this is the hardest and probably the most important factor in investment success.

"Let me give you an example of the need for patience. Many investors don't realize that from December 31, 1999 to December 31, 2009, the S&P 500 Index *lost* money. That's right, over those ten years, the index of the biggest U.S. companies – we're talking Apple, IBM, Microsoft, GM, Ford – had a negative total return. It takes great patience to stick with an asset class when you see those kinds of numbers."

"I didn't realize that," Paul said. "These days, the big U.S. tech companies are all the rage."

I nodded. "Because consistently following an investment approach is so critical, we know that a simple investment method that is easy to understand has a higher probability of success. That's why we like ACI…simple means the investor will find it easier to stick with it."

Paul chimed in, "You mean you follow the KISS approach, Keep It Simple Sir."

I smiled and nodded in agreement. But I could see that Donna was getting restless so I wanted to wrap up this part of the conversation quickly. Addressing her, I asked, "So Donna, we've covered the basics of what strategic asset investing is, why it matters and does it work. What do you see as the *benefits* of this approach?"

## Key Points

- Most investors want an investment approach that is understandable, efficient and effective.

- An "efficient" portfolio provides the best return for the corresponding amount of risk.

- An "inefficient" portfolio results primarily from high costs and human error. High taxes also make a portfolio inefficient.

- Multiple studies show asset class investing provides superior risk adjusted returns compared to market timing approaches:

  » 20-year study reveals that individual investors earn approximately 5%/year *less than* the S&P 500 Index. This is due mostly to behavior mistakes including loss aversion and following the herd mentality.

  » In second study of 100 pension plans, none that used market timing improved performance; most showed worse performance .

- » CALPERS has stopped using hedge funds (the kings of marketing timing).
- » S&P Company research shows that the majority of actively managed mutual funds underperform their benchmarks.
- » Investment newsletters don't consistently produce value
- "Market timing" is guessing the future direction (up or down) of a security or investment market.
- The time period used to measure results is critical and sometimes misleading.
- Following the three P's is key to successful investing:
  - » Persistence
  - » Perspective
  - » Patience.

**Notes:**

# CHAPTER 4 | The Benefits of Strategic Asset Class Investing

I waited for Donna to talk. She sat back and thought about my question on the benefits of asset class investing for a moment, then answered. "That's a question I've been asking myself. Let me see if I can answer. Well, first, asset class investing seems pretty simple to me. You divide your money into different buckets. You call these asset classes and they're investments that act differently from one another. The fact that it's simple makes it easier to understand and stick with, right? And fewer moving parts means less friction and wasted energy. It does seem to work from the information you shared.

"It's efficient from what I can see. It seems to require minimal effort and time on the part of the investor, but I do have some specific questions about how to do this.

"Also cost is a big deal with me and from what you say, asset class investing is less costly to implement.

"And the fact that we can stick with this approach is another benefit. We don't want to be switching advisers or trying to do this ourselves for a time and then giving up and going to someone else. I think you used the word, 'sustainable' earlier. That's definitely one of the elements that's a benefit to me. I want to be able to choose an approach and stick with it. We can avoid what Paul likes to call the 'bright shiny object' disease, right Paul?"

Paul added, "Right. I think you named most of the benefits I would have listed too… simple, effective, efficient and something we can stick with. Did we miss anything?"

I commented, "I think you hit most of the key points we touched on so far. I would add one benefit that we didn't really talk much about today, but we should mention it. It's *flexibility*. One of the great benefits about strategic asset class investing is that it works for any life situation. Whether an investor is just starting out like your oldest daughter, or the investor is mid-career like the two of you or if someone is approaching or even in retirement, we use the same approach. We even apply our approach to company sponsored retirement plans like your 401(k) plan, Donna, or the 403(b) plan you have at your school district, Paul. We like that a client can apply the principles of strategic asset class investing no matter what phase of life a client finds themselves in."

With that, our hour was up and I asked Donna and Paul how they would like to proceed.

Donna answered for them both and offered this idea, "Let us go away and think about what we've talked about today. It's been very, uh, let's say 'interesting' even though I hate that word. You've given us lots to think about and digest and I want to chew on this a bit. Okay with you Paul?"

Paul chirped back, "Okay with me too. Thanks Steve. You've been very helpful and I feel like I learned a lot that I didn't know about investing before." He stood up and offered his hand, "It's been fun," he grinned. Donna stood up too and asked, "Can we keep these charts and graphs you drew? It'll help me to remember what you were saying. How about if we give you a call in the next week after Paul and I have had time to talk?"

Pleased with the conversation, I agreed with them that this was a good next step and walked them out the door with a heartfelt thank you. As I went back to the conference room, I wondered what Donna and Paul would take away from the conversation. We covered a lot of ground, but they seemed to be involved and following. I was curious to see what they would do next.

## Key Points

- Strategic Asset Class Investing benefits:
  - » Simple
  - » Effective
  - » Efficient
  - » Sustainable
  - » Flexible.

## Notes:

# PART 2

# HOW TO PUT STRATEGIC ASSET CLASS INVESTING TO WORK

# The Players
# (aka the Circle Exercise)

About a week later, Donna and Paul sent me an email. Their note said that they appreciated all the time I was taking with them and they felt like they were learning a great deal about investing. They were pleased with that, but were not ready to commit to ACI investing just yet and wondered if I could give them another hour to go over what they called the "mechanics" of ACI. I guessed that this concern was coming mostly from Donna; Paul was skeptical, but I suspected that Donna is the family Chief Investment Officer (CIO). This request was fine with me, of course, because in order to for Paul and Donna to really buy into a new way to invest, they needed to understand it. I sent them a warm email response and we scheduled another session at our offices for later that week.

I was glad to see Paul and Donna when they came into the office and after settling in the conference room, Donna got down to business quickly. She started by saying, "We really appreciate your taking time with us to explain Strategic Asset Class Investing to us in a way we can understand so thank you for that." Paul nodded enthusiastically.

Donna continued, "And I went back home after our last meeting and looked up some of the studies you cited to prove that asset class investing usually beats other investment approaches. I found most of the studies you mentioned and a few more so we're convinced that this makes sense from an ROI standpoint, right Paul?" Again, Paul nodded as Donna went on, "But we want to know specifically how to put asset class investing to work for us. So today we'd like to know the nuts and bolts and see some real life examples if that's okay with you. I sent you an email on this. Did you get that?"

"Yes, I got that email," I replied, "And thanks for letting me know ahead of time so I could prepare some examples. And of course it's okay for us to go through how to invest this way. I know it's all new to you so there is much to learn."

Paul commented wryly, "Not so new anymore. I was telling Charles at work about this and he seemed skeptical. He said that this was fine if all I wanted was "average" returns. Funny thing though, I asked him about how his portfolio is doing and he told me that he fired his investment guy again because the guy was not doing much with his portfolio. That's the second or third time he's changed advisers since I've known him. And he sure seems to change around the investments in his 403(b) plan frequently.

"But Charles was quick to tell me about this hot stock that his new investment adviser had invested in for him. The adviser told him that this was an undervalued stock – I think he called it an 'undiscovered gem' – that was going to be the next Google. I thought that sounded a lot like market timing like we talked about last time. Charles is very excited and looks at the price of this stock all the time. He has it loaded on his phone so he can check it constantly. I sure don't want to spend my time that way."

I said, "I know what you mean. All that frantic activity. Reminds me of what Shakespeare said, 'full of sound and fury signifying nothing.' Not my cup of tea or how I want our clients to live either. Let me know what Charles says about that new stock and his new investment adviser.

"So today, let's do an exercise on paper to help you understand who the players are in the stage play of the investing world. This will help us to set the context for looking at how to create a strategic asset class portfolio and some examples. It will also help you to see where costs come from in managing a portfolio.

Don't worry, it's not like taking a test. This should be fun. Then I'll outline the five-step approach to implementing a Strategic Asset Class Investing approach. I want to talk a little more about passive investing versus active investing like your friend Charles is doing. Then we'll talk about the two ways to implement ACI, either do-it-yourself or done for you. At that point I can share with you three examples of actual portfolios some of our clients use. I also thought that it's time for us to talk about the downsides of ACI. It's not all smiles and roses you know. One of the downsides your friend Charles mentioned. Can you recall it?"

Paul jumped in quickly, "Sure. It bothered me when he said we would have to be okay with average performance. I don't know why, but that stuck in my mind."

Donna added, "What you've suggested all sounds fine. And you're good with us asking questions as we go along too, right? I kinda like the back and forth part of our discussions."

I responded, "Of course that's fine to ask questions as we go along. Remember, I talk about investing all day and I love it, so if I go too fast or don't explain something clearly, please stop me so I can cover what you need to know to understand fully. Let's get started. Here are two sheets of paper and you have pens, I see. Start by drawing a large circle in the middle of the page and put your names in the middle." They drew a circle that looked like this:

"You are the center of your investment universe." Paul chuckled and noted, "As it should be."

I continued, "Now what words can you put in the circle that describe your *mindset* around investing? Paul, what words would you put in the circle?"

Paul was quiet for a moment then said, "Hopeful, curious, fearful, determined, greedy and suspicious."

Donna added, "For me, it would be hopeful, yes, but also committed, scarcity, confused, suspicious, time-starved and maybe angry."

I said to Donna, "Why angry?"

She replied, "I'm a little angry that we've spent all this time and money investing for our kids' college and for our retirement and I feel like we've been wasting our time and our money. I feel like the investment advisers and mutual funds we've used have betrayed our trust. Until I started reading some of the research you gave us, I didn't realize how bad most investment advisers are. They don't tell us the truth, they don't work for us, they work for themselves, they charge high fees and they're just guessing about how to invest."

Paul and I looked at Donna and she said, "I'm sorry for that outburst. It just makes me mad to think that we're in our 50's now and we don't have that much time left before we need to start taking money out of our retirement accounts. We need to do better going forward. Okay, those are the words I'd put in my circle."

I nodded and said, "First Donna, thanks for sharing that. I hear that you're angry about how the financial industry has treated you up until now, right?" She nodded. "And second, it's very normal to be upset when you find out that most financial advisers and mutual fund companies are looking out for themselves and not their clients. I get it too. Your being angry is normal and understandable. So let's go ahead and write those words about your investing mindset around the inside of the circle." Paul and Donna did so – Paul's was kind of haphazard and Donna was more precise.

"Now I want you to list three financial goals on the inside of the circle: one short, one medium and one long term. Just jot down the key words here. You can go back and clean this up later. Do this separately first and don't show the other one your work." Donna and Paul nodded and slightly turned away from each other and covered their papers. I could see they were starting to get into this.

"Please share your work with each other." I waited as they exchanged papers and scanned the others' paper. When they looked up, I asked "Any comments or surprises on what you see on the other person's paper?"

Paul, the ever quick to speak one, said, "The first thing I noticed is that we have some similar goals and a couple of different ones too. We agree that the long-term goal is to save for retirement. But we have different short and medium term goals. Is that normal?"

I answered, "Yes, that's pretty typical for couples. Donna, thoughts or comments?"

She offered, "I'm not surprised we have the same long term goal to save for retirement because we talk about that sometimes. But I was surprised that Paul listed owning a cabin as a medium term goal." Turning to Paul she continued, "I know you talk about that sometimes, but I didn't know you wanted one that badly. And I was surprised that you did not list a kitchen remodel as a goal. We've talked about it and I thought you wanted that too."

Paul responded, "The kitchen remodel is *your* goal and I'm happy to go along, but I really want that cabin in the woods someday. Someplace we can escape to and where we can all meet as a family and I can take my buddies for fishing and hiking." Paul and Donna looked at each other and I could see the spark of affection go between them. Honestly sharing goals with a partner does that sometimes.

I said, "Remember that money is just energy that we use to reach our life goals. It's a medium of exchange. You work to earn money in exchange for your work and you exchange money for a kitchen remodel or to buy a cabin in the woods. Money is not good, or evil and does not have any value in itself. Having more money is not the goal…it's having the life you want and money just helps you get there.

"Okay, thanks for sharing your goals and for being so honest with one another and for letting me in on your mindsets. Paul, you look like you want to say something here. Spit it out my man."

Paul smiled and said, "You know, our current adviser and none of the advisers we've ever used have asked us about our goals this way. And none of them have ever talked about money like this with us. Not to give you too big of a head, but that's different and I like it."

"Thanks Paul. I won't let it get to my head. But that's why we start a discussion about the investment environment like this. The two of you are the center of your money universe, as you should be, and you bring a certain mindset to the process and have life goals that we need to know about. Otherwise, investing is an academic exercise, and I want it to be real for you. So give each other back the papers and please talk about your goals when you go home.

"Moving on to your circles. In the lower left hand side, draw another circle and write in the word 'custodian.' A custodian is a financial institution that holds a customer's securities for safe-keeping. Charles Schwab, Fidelity, TD Ameritrade and Vanguard are custodians."

Paul interrupted, "But I have some Fidelity mutual funds in my 403(b) and Donna has Vanguard mutual funds too."

"It's confusing I know," I replied. "All these firms make money in many ways including selling their own mutual funds, acting as custodians, even being a bank in a couple of cases. But we want to think of them as custodians for now. The thing to keep in mind is that these custodians are all pretty much the same. Like grocery stores. We can buy bread, soup, butter and milk at any grocery store. Some of them sell their own brand of products as well as national brands. They're good at being custodians and can charge a very low fee to arrange the buying and selling of securities. They all charge about the same for most transactions, about $9 or so for each security order to buy or sell if you do it yourself. So that's the custodian. They hold the securities you buy.

Donna and Paul were following so I pushed on. "In the upper left corner of your paper, draw another circle and write the words 'mutual funds/ETFs' inside it. You probably know what a mutual fund is but you might not know what an ETF is so let me explain a little. 'ETF' stands for 'exchange traded fund' and an ETF is similar to a mutual fund in that it holds a basket of stocks or bonds, but it's different in a one key way. A mutual fund is priced (and traded) at the end of the day and an ETF is traded by the moment like a stock. From a tax standpoint, an ETF is often more efficient because an ETF usually doesn't accumulate capital gains the way a mutual fund does.

"On the other hand, because it trades like a stock, an ETF can have sudden ups and downs due to buyers and sellers not being in alignment. However, we usually don't care about this because we enter market orders to buy and sell so sudden changes in prices should not affect us. A big advantage of an ETF is that it is usually cheaper to own overall than a mutual fund. Most mutual fund companies offer ETFs as well as mutual funds that own the same thing. Vanguard, for example, offers investors mutual funds and ETFs that track the same indexes.

"When you enter an order to buy a mutual fund or ETF, the custodian makes the trade and holds it in your account for you. Any questions so far about custodians or mutual fund companies?"

"No, we're following," said Donna.

I continued, "For the last circle, in the upper right part of the paper, draw another circle and put the word 'adviser' there with a question mark." Their finished circles looked like this:

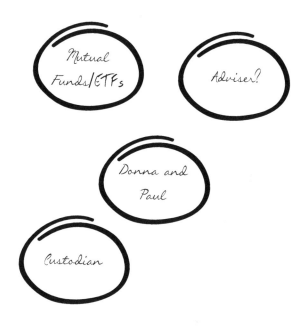

I think that's pretty self-explanatory, but I want to talk a little about the different kinds of advisers there are. My company produced a white paper titled "How Advisers Get Paid and Why It Matters" that you can get from our website (www.finpath.com/money-matters) if you want, but here is a summary of what that paper says.

"There are basically four types of advisers." I wrote these words on a pad of paper that I had in front of me and pushed it into the middle of the table so Donna and Paul could see:

Commission

Commission and fee

Salary and bonus

Fee-only

"The first is **a commissioned salesperson that makes money when the investor buys a product.** Think of an insurance salesman who sells you insurance or an annuity. The second type of adviser is one who **gets paid both commissions and fees.** This is the way most financial advisers are paid. This type of financial adviser receives commissions for products and may also receive fees for certain services. Representatives from Edward Jones, Ameriprise and Merrill Lynch operate this way.

"Representatives who work for discount brokerage firms are the third type of adviser. They are usually paid **a salary and a bonus.** The reps at Fidelity, Schwab and TD Ameritrade are paid this way."

Paul interrupted, "But these are also custodians, right? Do the people who work as these custodians get paid when we use them? I'm confused."

I answered, "Remember I said that these financial companies have many businesses? Here is an example, besides being custodians of your accounts, these companies can also make money by selling you other services or convincing you to buy their in-house mutual funds or even insurance and annuities in some cases. These big financial companies will do almost anything to sell you more services and products. And their sales people are really good at it. Their pay is based on their ability to get you buy more from them. As long as you know this, it's fine, but most investors don't realize it.

"The **fourth way** advisers are paid is called 'fee-only' and that's how we get paid. A fee-only adviser is paid by their client for the services they provide. She doesn't sell products or get commissions. Some fee-only advisers are paid a percentage of their client's assets, and others are paid hourly, by the project or even a retainer-type of flat fee."

Paul chimed in, "I was wondering how someone goes about finding a fee-only adviser like you. I was telling a friend who works in the Mid-West that we were going to sit down with you and he asked." I answered, "I suggest that your friend look for a fee-only adviser through the Garrett Planning Network (www.garrettplan-ningnetwork.com). It's one of the professional groups I belong to and in my opinion the best group of fee-only advisers." Paul nodded and made a note.

I continued, "So that's the investing environment. How much of that is new and do you have any questions before we move on to constructing a strategic asset class portfolio? Take a look at your completed circles and let's cover anything that is confusing for you."

Most people have lots of questions when I give them this over-view and I was curious to see what Donna and Paul would say. I was not disappointed. Donna chimed in first, "I didn't know most of what you described so thanks for giving us the lay of the land. I always wondered how Fidelity could both have mutual funds and hold my accounts too. Seems like kind of a conflict of interest to me."

"It is a conflict of interest and they have internal rules to manage that, but it's sure not clear to investors, " I responded. "But now you know. What else?"

"The information about how advisers are paid is kinda scary to me," Donna said. "I knew that our insurance guy always tells us he has ideas for retirement too, but now I know why. He gets paid if we buy investments from him, but I didn't consider him on the same plane as our investment adviser, or you for that matter."

Paul chimed in by saying, "Our investment adviser tells me that he is 'fee-based.' Is that the same thing as fee-only? He seems to suggest it's the same, but hearing your explanation, I wonder."

"They aren't the same thing, as you suspected, Paul," I said. "And here is something else to keep in mind; a **fee-only adviser** isn't a representative of any other company and gets paid only by clients. A **fee-based adviser** gets paid by the company she or he works for and their first loyalty is to their employer. Keep in mind that this doesn't make them a bad person or a poor adviser; it just means that they work for their company and not you. A fee-only adviser works only for you and their other clients."

"I'm glad to hear that you're a fee-only adviser, Steve," Donna offered. "Seems like that means we get better unbiased information and advice."

"Thank you, Donna," I said nodding. "We think so, but keep in mind I have my biases too. For example, I believe the best way to invest is to follow the strategic asset class approach.

"Okay, now that you an idea of the various players with an investor is involved, shall we get into how we go about co-creating a portfolio for investors? We can come back to this financial environment topic if you want later, but I think you're anxious to see how this works and I'm anxious to show you. Ready to push on?"

Donna and Paul both nodded and I proceeded. "Put your circle exercises aside and let's get into how to create a reliable ROI for your investments."

## Key Points:

Four major players on the investment landscape:

- » Commission for selling products
- » Commission and fee for selling products and providing services
- » Salary and bonus to provide services
- » Fee-only, may offer broad or narrow range of services; paid only by client.

## Notes:

# Five Steps to a Strategic Asset Class Portfolio

"With that as a background, let me show you how we go about creating a strategic asset allocation portfolio," I offered. "You understand that the goal here is **not** to create *your* portfolio, but to give you an idea of how the process works. Okay?"

Donna and Paul nodded and I continued. "Albert Einstein said 'everything should be made as simple as possible, but not simpler' and that's our goal with creating a portfolio – simple and effective. Like Paul's KISS comment earlier.

"There are five steps in creating a strategic asset class portfolio. Here is a simple diagram of the process:

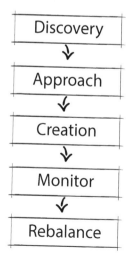

"We're not going to go through all five steps in detail today. I just want to hit the highlights to give you an idea of the key points. Okay with you?"

Donna replied, "Yes, that makes sense. If we want more details, we can get them later."

Paul nodded and I continued, "Sure. There are several good books on the subject and my company even created a summary called 'Strategic Asset Class Investing Overview' that you can get from our website (www.finpath.com/money-matters) if you're interested. Okay, briefly the first two steps.

"Discovery is just what it sounds like. The investor needs to be clear about her or his goals, time horizon for those goals, risk tolerance, how much of a loss they can handle without abandoning ship and other pertinent information.

"Establishing the investor's overall investment approach is the next step and it has two main outcomes: setting expectations and choosing the investment classes the investor will use in her portfolio." Pulling out a chart, I said, "Here are the asset classes to choose from. Of course, not all clients use all asset classes." This is the list I showed them:

- Stocks
- Bonds
- REITs
- Commodities/Natural Resources
- Private Equity
- Private Debt
- Direct Investment Commercial Real Estate

- Direct Investment Residential Real Estate
- Cash

Paul looked up from the list and said, "We don't have to own all of these, right? I'm not even sure what private equity and private debt are. And commodities make me nervous." Donna nodded thoughtfully and added, "And what about small company stocks, international stocks and gold and silver?"

I answered, "We subdivide some of these asset classes to **diversify within the asset class**. Small company U.S. stocks and stocks from the emerging markets are usually added to the mix. We don't believe in precious metals as assets because gold and silver don't produce income and just sit there. The price of precious metals goes up and down based purely on investor fear. Remember that when we first talked about asset classes there were a number of items that are not assets in our minds: gold, silver, collectibles like coins, stamps and art, and bottles of wine. Your house isn't either, of course. "

I continued, "How about if you put a star next to the asset classes you might use if you were creating a new portfolio for you?"

Donna marked three asset classes and I put an "X" next to one more. Here was the list after we'd both written on it:

- Stocks*
- Bonds*
- REITs*
- Commodities/Natural Resources
- Private Equity
- Private Debt

- Direct Investment Commercial Real Estate
- Direct Investment Residential Real Estate
- Cash X

I commented, "I added cash because it's almost impossible to not have cash in a portfolio and it's a different asset class. This list is what a typical client might start with. You have four primary asset classes to use in creating a strategic asset class portfolio. There would probably be a few more sub-classes added, but this would be the end of this step.

I pulled the diagram back into the middle of the table so Paul and Donna could see, and pointed to it. "Here's where we are in the design process."

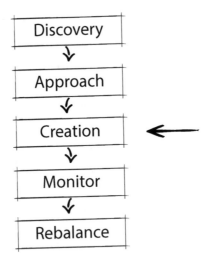

"In this third step, the investor creates her portfolio. She does this by choosing how much of her portfolio to put into each of the asset classes. Take a look at this table." I slid this chart in front of them.

**U.S. Stock & Bond Market January 1, 1990 to December 31, 2015**

| | Portfolio | Average Annual Return | Best Year | Worst Year |
|---|---|---|---|---|
| A | 100% Equities | 10.3% | 37.6% | -37.0% |
| B | 80% Stocks/20% Bonds | 9.6% | 34.8% | -25.6% |
| C | 60% Stocks/40% Bonds | 8.9% | 31.9% | -14.2% |
| D | 50% Stocks/50% Bonds | 8.5% | 30.5% | -8.5% |
| E | 40% Stocks/60% Bonds | 8.2% | 29.1% | -4.3% |
| F | 20% Stocks/80% Bonds | 7.4% | 26.3% | -6.2% |
| G | 100% Bonds | 6.7% | 23.5% | -11.1% |

Source: PocketRisk using Morningstar data. Disclaimer: Past performance is not a guarantee of future experience. Investment returns will differ from the information shown here.

Paul and Donna leaned forward and studied the numbers. Continuing, I said, "As you know, past performance is no guarantee of future results, but if we assume the next 15 years are like the past 15, which portfolio would best suit your desired level of risk and return?"

After a minute, Paul chimed in, "I'm definitely a 'C'. What about you Donna?" Donna, the more thoughtful of the two said, "I'm probably more of a 'D' or 'E' person. I'll bet you see lots of couples who don't agree on this, right?"

I laughed, "Yes. I can't think of the last time a couple did this exercise and their choices were exactly the same. Keeping in mind the overall target portfolio the investor chose from this exercise, she or he will then divide their portfolio among the asset classes they chose. It might look like this to start:"

| ASSET CLASS | % |
|---|---|
| Large U.S. Stocks | 20 |
| Small U.S. Stocks | 20 |
| Non- U.S. Stocks | 10 |
| REITs | 10 |
| U.S. Bonds | 25 |
| Non-U.S. Bonds | 10 |
| Cash | 5 |

"We'd call this a 60/40 portfolio because it has 60% stocks and 40% fixed-income. It's a moderate portfolio that you might see lots of mid-career people have. Then the investor would go to a free website and create a model portfolio. If they were working with us, we would do it for them. We'd create two more portfolios too – one more aggressive and one more conservative for the client to see alternatives. This is a bit of a trial and adjust process. Questions so far?"

Donna leaned back and said, "No that seems pretty clear. The investor looks at historical returns and losses, chooses the one she's most comfortable with and then divides her portfolio into the asset classes she chose to use, right?"

"You got it," I said. "If you want to see how you are currently invested from an asset allocation standpoint, we created a do it yourself worksheet that you can download from our website (www.finpath.com/money-matters)." Donna and Paul both nodded and made a note.

"All that's left are the last two items in the process. The investor will want to monitor the performance of her portfolio over time, that's step four in this process." Paul looked like he wanted to say something so I paused and looked at him. "Paul?"

Obligingly, he asked, "How often does an investor want to do that? I have friends that look at their portfolios daily and that seems like way too much."

In response, I said, "We like to see investors being a little more thoughtful and disciplined about looking at their investments. For most investors, three or four times a year is enough. Performance monitoring allows the investor to know what's going on with their portfolio on a regular basis and thereby be informed. We find that an informed investor is one less likely to panic and make sudden changes."

Donna looked amused and said, "I can see the value of that. Paul and I tend to ignore our investments most of the time and only look at our statements when the markets are going down. We don't really know what's going on most of the time. But I don't want to look too often either. I figure we just keep saving and that's the best thing we can do." She shifted in her seat and said, "Okay, got it so far. What about making changes in a portfolio? I hear the term 'buy and hold' sometimes. If an investor is not a market timer, is that what she's doing if she uses asset class investing?"

"Not really," I responded. "True 'buy and hold' means an investor makes a decision about her portfolio mix and then never changes it. While we don't believe in market timing, as you know, we don't believe in pure 'buy and hold' either. We use something that's in

between and that comes into play in the last step called 'rebalancing.'"
I pointed to the last box on the diagram.

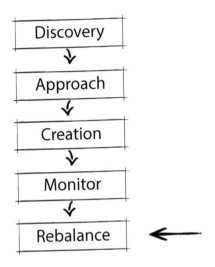

I wanted to finish the last step in the process while Paul and Donna were still with me. "Remember when the investor chose how to divide her money among the asset classes when she created her portfolio? She used a target percentage for each asset class, maybe 15% for large U.S. stocks, 5% for REITs or 30% for U.S. bonds. Well, what happens over time to the percentage that is in each of those asset classes?"

Paul answered, "Some of the asset classes have more in them than the targets and some have less. Plus, most investors are saving money like Donna said so there is more cash in the portfolio, right?"

I nodded, "Yes, that's right on both counts, Paul. And keep in mind that some investors are taking money out of their accounts too. That won't be something you need to worry about for a few years, but withdrawals are another way the target percentages can change over time. When the investor sets the target percentage for each asset class, she also sets the range that will trigger a rebalance. When the percentage of an asset class gets too high, the investor sells some of that asset and reinvests the money back into an asset class that is lower than its target number."

Paul shifted in his seat and started to say something, but then stopped. I knew that he wanted to ask a question and could guess what his question was. I looked at him, but he waved for me to continue. The question would come out soon enough, I thought.

I finished: "Rebalancing is the way an investor returns her portfolio back to the targets."

Donna was thoughtful and asked, "How often are portfolios rebalanced."

"In our experience, maybe once or twice a year," I said. "Some years not at all." Paul couldn't stand it anymore and broke in. "Wait a minute," he said. "Do I understand that you're going to be selling asset classes that are doing well and reinvesting that money into ones that are doing poorly? Did I hear that right?"

I laughed and said, "You got that right. This is one of the harder concepts for someone new to strategic asset class investing to grasp—the investor is selling winners and buying losers." I wrote the words on the page:

Sell winners and buy losers!

"You've both heard the old saying that a smart investor should buy low and sell high, right?" They both nodded. "In our experience, very few investors do this. Investors get caught up in the emotion of seeing a stock or security go up and they like the feeling of having a 'winner'. There are so many problems with this emotional response I don't know where to start, but suffice it to say that almost no one buys low and sells high. It's usually just the opposite. Disciplined rebalancing is the only way I know to make sure an investor sells high and buys low."

Paul sat back and shook his head. Meanwhile, Donna added, "You know Paul, that's what happened with that tech stock you bought, what was the name of that? Anyway, you bought it because Charles told you about it and you watched it go up and were so excited. Then it started to go down and you couldn't sell it because you kept telling me that it would come back. You know what? It never came back and the company got acquired at a price that was $10 or $12 per share less than what you paid for it. That's the perfect example of buy high and sell low."

Paul smiled and said, "Yes, I learned my lesson on that one. No more for me. Luckily we didn't lose that much, but I get what you're saying, Steve. It's easy to get caught up in the thrill of a rising stock price." He had a rueful look on his face and said, "So rebalancing is a way to make sure we stick with the buy low and sell high idea, right?"

"Yes, pretty much," I said. "It's easy to say, but hard to do.

"Okay, that pretty much wraps up the 'how to do asset class investing' discussion. Did we leave anything out?"

Donna replied, "We didn't talk about choosing specific securities did we? And I have a nagging question about whether we can do this ourselves or if – maybe I should say 'how much'– help we're going to need. Can we talk about those?"

I stood up to stretch and said, "Yes, of course we can talk about both of those questions. How about a little break first? Need some coffee or water?" They both stood up and Paul said, "I could use a refill. How about you Donna?"

## Key Points:

Five steps to a Strategic Asset Allocation Portfolio:

1. Discovery:
    a. Investor's goals

    a. Risk and loss tolerance

    a. Constraints/Preferences

2. Investment Approach:
    a. Set frame of reference for returns and benchmark

    b. Choose asset classes to use

3. Portfolio Creation:
    a. Divide money into asset classes by percentage

    a. Test options

    a. Implement

4. Monitor Performance:
    a. Regular **scheduled** reviews

    b. Purpose: determine if asset classes are within target ranges

5. Rebalance:
    a. Purpose: reallocate dollars if needed

    a. "Sell winners and buy losers!"

Active and Passive Investing

Paul and Donna returned looking refreshed and with fresh coffee to fuel them. They seemed eager to continue and I was curious to hear what questions they would ask before we dug in again. They sat down and Donna started with, "I think I understand most of how to create an asset class portfolio and I really like that asset class investing is simple and time efficient. I can think of better ways for us to spend time than working on our investments. Well, maybe not *better*, but at least something I like to do more. But there is one thing we haven't talked much about. How does an investor choose mutual funds or stocks or whatever they're going to use for the asset classes they want to use in their portfolio?"

I replied, "Logical next question to answer, Donna. Remember that we used the terms 'active' and 'passive' investing earlier? The investment world is divided into these two separate camps. Think of it this way. Say you're flying over a forest and look down. Active investing is trying to pick out the few trees that will outgrow the others and switching frequently when that approach doesn't work. Market timing is a form of active investing. There are many other kinds of active investing, but that gives you the idea.

"On the other hand, a passive investing philosophy

means buying the whole forest. Asset class investing is the investment approach to put this philosophy into practice. Using passive mutual funds and ETFs is the way to implement asset class investing. Here's a way to visualize it." I drew this diagram for them:

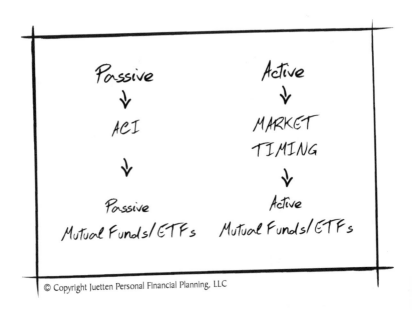

Paul jumped in again, "Okay, that makes sense. I was really struck by your comment that it's impossible to predict the future with any degree of certainty. That's what active management is, right? I think that's what you mean by 'guessing' with our portfolio."

"That's exactly what I mean, Paul. Investment markets are very efficient – not perfectly efficient – but very efficient. It's almost as if everyone that is looking at a forest knows the same facts about the forest: what kind of trees grow there, what the soil is like, how much rain there's been, how fast a certain type of tree grows in general and so forth. But choosing the specific trees that are going to grow the fastest in the future is just about impossible.

"Charles Ellis, we talked about his data before, wrote a book about the perils of market timing. The title is, *Winning the Loser's Game*, and in it he argues that market timing is a loser's game. He said that the only way to win a loser's game is not to play. I like that idea. With asset class investing, we aren't playing the loser's game."

Paul commented, "There's that word 'efficient' again. Efficient portfolio, efficient from a time standpoint like Donna said and efficient investment markets. What are you, an 'efficiency expert'?" He grinned at me and I knew he was kidding me.

Donna spoke up and said, "I agree about not playing the loser's game and I get the point about choosing the whole forest and not a few trees. But what *vehicles* does an investor use to buy the forest? It's mutual funds, right?"

I shifted towards Donna and settled in. "Right, we use mostly passive mutual funds and ETFs and sometimes we even have to use actively traded mutual funds." Donna looked confused and Paul cocked his head in a way that I knew he was confused too.

Donna said with a touch of annoyance, "Just when I think I'm following, you throw that in. Okay, I get that asset class investing is passive and not active and it would make sense to use passive vehicles to implement the asset class approach. But what do you mean sometimes you suggest active mutual funds or ETFs?"

I chuckled and replied, "I understand your confusion, but let me ask you one thing: how many passive funds do you and Paul have available in your 401(k) plan and his 403(b) plan?"

Donna nodded, "Not many in mine, what about you Paul?"

Paul replied while looking at the statements he had brought along, "Here are the investment choices in my plan. I don't know what all of these are. How can I tell if they're active or passive?"

"May I take a look?" I asked. Paul slid the papers over to me. "Hmmm," I said. You have many fund choices and it looks like there are no passive funds in your lineup. For example, an index fund is passive and you don't seem to have any of those."

Donna said, "I didn't bring my list, but I think we have some index funds. I recall seeing those when I looked last time. So index funds are passive then?"

"Yes," I replied. "Index funds are passive and now you can see why I say we sometimes have to use actively managed mutual funds. Paul's plan doesn't seem to have any index funds in it and many employer plans are like that. The typical investor may have to choose the least offensive mutual fund in his or her employer plan."

Paul muttered, "I always thought the District's investment options were not that great."

"So whenever possible we use passive mutual funds and ETFs, but as you can see with Paul's plan options at his work, we don't always have a choice. But usually we can figure out the best options in a limited universe, like with Paul's employer."

Donna queried me further, "Can you give me some idea of the funds an investor might use?"

"Sure," I said. "But first, do you remember what an ETF is?"

Paul nodded faintly and not at all confidently and Donna shook her head and said. "Some, but remind me."

I replied, "An **Exchange Traded Fund or ETF** is like a mutual fund in that it holds a basket of underlying individual stocks or bonds. Like mutual funds, ETFs are regulated by the SEC, but it's different than a mutual fund because it trades like a stock every minute an exchange is open. A mutual fund is bought and sold <u>at the end of the day</u> and an investor buys or sells an ETF <u>during the day</u>.

"ETFs were first created in the 1990's and have become very popular. There are market timing ETFs and passive ETFs, just like there are market timing and passive mutual funds. And here are some other differences between an ETF and mutual funds besides the ones I've described so far:

- Operating costs for ETFs are usually (but not always) lower compared to mutual funds

- ETFs can have sudden swings in price up or down due to market swings during the day

- They tend to be more tax-efficient than mutual funds

- ETFs trade with a bid/ask spread whereas mutual funds simply trade at the market price." I extended my arms and put one hand higher than the other. "Bid/ask spread means there is a difference between what the owner is asking for to sell something and what the potential owner is bidding to buy the item." I put my hands down again and continued. "Imagine you owned an antique chair that I wanted to buy. You are asking $100 for the chair and I'm willing to pay $95 for it. The bid/ask spread is $5. An ETF bid/ask spread can be small – a penny or two a share – or large—five to ten cents.

"You can find a good education piece on ETFs at the SEC

website (www.sec.gov)."

"Now can we get to some specific examples please?" Donna asked.

Happy to dive into specifics, I wrote these names on a piece of paper and said, "Here are the names of mutual funds and ETFs we recommend. Recognize any?"

| Mutual Funds | ETFs |
|---|---|
| DFA | Vanguard |
| Vanguard | iShares |
| Fidelity | PowerShares |
| Schwab | |

Donna said, "I see Vanguard mutual funds advertised a lot. I didn't know they have ETFs too. And I know the Fidelity and Schwab names. I think Fidelity has something to do with our 401(k) plan. Paul?"

He nodded, "Same for me. But we don't use Fidelity in our 403(b) plan. We use someone else. I'm confused though; why would Vanguard have both mutual funds and ETFs?"

I replied, "Remember when we talked about the players in the game earlier? I shared that financial companies have many ways that they make money. They can be custodians, sell products like mutual funds and ETFs and even be a 401(k) record keeper like Fidelity does for Donna's 401(k) plan. This is one of the dirty little secrets in the financial world. All of these big companies are trying to sell as many services as they can because once they get an investor used to them, they can sell more services and products."

Paul, the somewhat cynical one, added, "It's like our car insurance company isn't it? Our agent is always trying to sell us more kinds of insurance, even when we don't need it."

"Yes, that's a good comparison, Paul," I agreed. "But that doesn't mean their services aren't any good. You just need to remember that they are in the business of selling you products and services and you have to remember who's on your side.

"We recommend the best mutual funds or ETFs for a client depending on where they already invest their money. If a client uses Fidelity or Schwab as their custodian, we can recommend Vanguard ETFs or sometimes a Schwab or Fidelity ETF. We can buy ETFs at any of them."

Donna tossed in a question. "I see that you listed 'DFA' as the first mutual fund. What is that and why list it first? I've never heard of them."

I replied, "Many investors have not heard of them either. DFA stands for Dimensional Fund Advisors (www.dfaus.com) and it's a company that offers a unique kind of mutual fund. Their mutual funds are passive, but they build the funds to add some additional return by sticking to a famous model developed by academics from the University of Chicago and Dartmouth. They created 'super index funds' that are often better than straight index funds. We use their mutual funds for some of our client's accounts. I can tell you more if you're interested. But for now, the key thing to keep in mind is that all of these vehicles are passive. We don't believe in market timing and so we don't recommend market timing vehicles like active mutual funds. How's that?"

Paul nodded and asked, "I gather from what we've talked about last time and today that most people use market timing instead of passive investing? Why do so much of the media and most advisers focus on market timing? And why do so many investors listen?"

Donna jumped in, "I think I know the answer to the first question. Hype sells, doesn't it?"

I nodded. "That's right. Remember that the media is all about selling products and to get your attention, they need to be hyping the next great thing. And keep in mind that most advisers have to justify their fees by appearing to add value. If you make something seem hard and mysterious, you can charge more for it. The typical adviser is making money by selling snake oil. It doesn't mean they're bad people, just selling something inferior. Remember, most people who call themselves financial advisers are just salespeople.

"The 'smart money' like big pension funds and informed individual investors focus on being efficient and effective. They focus on not making mistakes and using time wisely. I know that's important to you both." They nodded.

I continued. "And to answer Paul's second question, why do you think it's hard to be a passive investor and many investors listen to the guesses that market 'experts' make about the future of investments? Let's list some reasons."

This time Donna wrote on the pad, "Let's see. First, we want to follow the herd and be like everyone else." She wrote the word "herd" on the pad as she continued, "We want to be in control and it seems like making lots of trades is being in control, although it's not as we've found out, right, Paul?"

He nodded and added, "Write down 'competitive' on the list too. It may be more of guy thing, but a bunch of people at work are always bragging about their hot stock picks, like Charles. We want to be winners and passive investing seems like it's settling for 'average,' although from the chart you showed us, 'average' returns are better than about 80% of market timers in any one year."

Donna was writing and nodding her agreement as Paul talked and said, "Don't forget all the media attention investing gets. I see CNBC or one of those 24-7 TV channels on all the time when I'm out in public. And investing discussions seem to be all over the Internet too. It's hard to ignore it sometimes."

I added, "And it seems to be in our nature to want to try to predict the future. We listen to weather forecasts, try to guess who's going to win the Super Bowl and I noticed that there is even estimated drive time on the freeway signs now. It just seems like we as human beings like to try to guess what's going to happen next. Maybe it has something to do with our survival instinct or something."

Paul nodded in agreement and said, "Yes, like watching out for danger in the future. But since the future is unknowable as you like to tell us, investing based on guesses seems like a bad plan."

Donna was nodding and writing as Paul and I talked. I looked over and here is what Donna's pad looked like:

*Herd*

*Control*

*Competition*

*Average*

*Media*

I looked at her list. Donna continued, "Okay, so I get that asset class investing uses passive mutual funds and ETFs most of the time. Active investing uses active mutual funds and most of them use market timing. Still, I keep wondering if we can do this ourselves or do we need help. You're an adviser, but I trust you, Steve. What do you say?"

"Good question and let's get to that next."

**Key Points:**

- Active investing involves ongoing buying and selling by an investor in an attempt to take advantage of perceived opportunities. Research shows most active investing fails over time.

- Passive investing limits buying and selling to reduce costs and avoid mistakes; a passive investor avoids guessing about the future (which is unknowable anyway).

- Investment markets are very efficient – everyone has access to the same information.

- **Strategic Asset Class Investing** is a passive investment approach and uses passive investment vehicles (index mutual funds and ETFs).

- An ETF is similar to a mutual fund in some ways, but trades like a stock during the day rather than at the end of the day; has other advantages over mutual funds.

- Providers of passive vehicles include DFA, Vanguard, iShares, Fidelity, Schwab.

- Why so much focus on market timing by the press and most advisers?

  » Hype gets attention and attention sells more products.

  » Most advisers are not giving advice … they are **salespeople.**

**Notes:**

# CHAPTER 8

# DIY or Done For You?

"As a backdrop to answering your question about doing it yourself versus using an adviser, Donna, let's take another brief look at the investment landscape," I said. **"Investing is simple, but not easy.** You'll hear me say this a few times today. It's simple because successful investing requires following a few basic principles like the ones we've discussed. That's what we have with strategic asset class investing – a few basic principles distilled into a system that anyone can follow.

"But successful investing is hard for a few reasons. First, because the future is unknowable, **investing for the future brings with it uncertainty that can't be avoided.** Even if you have a solid investment plan, there will be uncertainty and many investors have a difficult time dealing with the uncertainty. As you know from our discussions about the risk and return curve, uncertainty has the potential to deliver rewards too, but many investors forget that when their investments are going down. Too often they panic."

Donna and Paul nodded seriously. "Second, investing is simple, but not easy because **the investor can easily get distracted by all the noise that surrounds investing.** Here's a picture of what the investment world looks like." I drew this diagram:

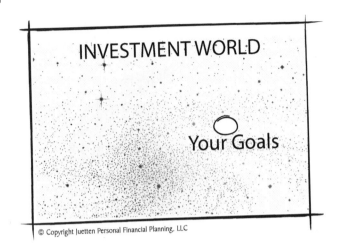

"As we've discussed, the financial media is everywhere and your friends and co-workers like to talk about investment items too. **The only goals that matters are yours, but there's all this noise.** It's a little like standing in the middle of a casino and listening to the slot machines making that 'ka-ching, bing, bing, bing' sound. You **know** the people hitting the slot machine buttons are losing all their money in the long run, but there's something alluring and intoxicating about all the sound and flashing lights, isn't there?"

Paul grinned and said, "You got that right. And you think to yourself, 'that could be me!' Donna and I go to a casino about once a year and I always come away a little overwhelmed by the whole thing."

Donna chimed in, "I like the shows, but still manage to feed a few dollars into the slots for fun. But I know what you mean about investing too. There is so much noise about it if you pay attention to it. I try to ignore most of the noise."

"Good for you," I said, "But it's hard to ignore, especially when something dramatic happens. And the last reason investing is hard is because **the financial industry is set up to separate you from your money and transfer it into their pockets.** No one in the financial industry – not even me – cares as much about your money as you do. The industry is really good at convincing you that they are interested in you while charging you high fees and most investors are not aware of how this happens and what they can do about it."

Donna offered, "Okay, I think we get that investing is simple, but not easy, but the question still remains. Can an investor do this themselves or does the investor need help and, if so, how much and what kind? All the information you've shared about the financial industry scare me a bit. Paul and I have wondered about our current investment adviser and others we've worked with; we always had an uneasy feeling that maybe we weren't getting the full story."

I answered Donna with my own question, "Remember I told you that we believe that once you have a sound investment plan there are three keys to a successful investment program?" Paul answered, "Sure, the three 'P's' you called them: Persistence, Perspective and Patience."

"Right you are, Paul," I said, "Consistently practicing these three behaviors will make anyone a successful investor if they have a time proven investment philosophy to follow. So assuming an investor follows a good investment plan – and we believe it's the strategic asset class investing approach – and can use the three 'P's,' an investor can be successful with either DIY or Done for You. I've seen both work. Let's look at the elements of a successful Do It Yourself investment approach first.

"To be successful as a DIY investor, you need five attributes," I said, and I pulled the pad towards me and wrote on the left side:

## DIY

Time

Interest

Minimal math

Discipline

Emotional maturity

"You need to have the *time* to manage your investment consistently. As Will Rogers said, 'Even if you're on the right track, you'll get run over if you just stand there.'

Next, the successful DIY investor must also be *interested* in investing. I know many smart people who aren't interested in learning enough about investing to be successful. Time and interest seem to go hand-in-hand too. If an investor is interested in investing, she will make the time. Of course, there is *minimal math* required, but most of the numbers are pretty basic. And with good computer programs now available, even the math is getting easier.

"The last two requirements are tricky because they involve human emotion. *Discipline* is needed to regularly review a portfolio and stick with the rebalancing process. Selling high and buying low as we preach is not an easy thing to do, right Paul?" He grinned and nodded. "And seeing the long view, the big picture and avoiding the instant gratification that we all seem to crave requires *emotional maturity*. We are often our own worst enemies." Donna and Paul nodded agreement.

"So what are the elements of successful investing using an adviser? We'll call this the Done for You or DFY approach." I wrote these words on the pad next to the DIY column.

| DIY | DFY |
|---|---|
| Time | Trust |
| Interest | Good communications |
| Minimal math | Clear expectations |
| Discipline | Understand costs |
| Emotional maturity | Fiduciary |

"Trust in your adviser is essential if you're going the DFY approach," I started out. Steven Covey says that trust is made up of two parts: competence and character. A successful investor must carefully investigate any adviser she is considering to determine if they are trustworthy. There is an easy way to determine competence: ask an adviser about their training, educational background and professional education. I'm surprised how few people ask me about my credentials."

"Initials after a person's name may not mean much. There are something like 90 different designations that a financial person can have. Some are useful and others are not. For example, I'm a CERTIFIED FINANCIAL PLANNER™ practitioner or "CFP®" professional for short. It's widely viewed as the gold standard of professional designations in this field and there are some other designations that are useful, but most are not. A 'CFP®' practitioner designation behind an adviser's name means she has passed seven or so college-level classes on financial matters, passed a lengthy exam and has worked under the supervision of a working CFP® professional for a few years and agrees to follow a strict code of ethics.

"The character part of trust is not easy to judge or even to define. Basically, I think character comes down to doing what you say you're going to do and acting in good faith. We'll touch on that in a minute.

"Also, good two-way communication is essential if an investor is going to use an adviser. Most financial advisers are good **sales people**, but an investor has to ask herself, 'Does this person really listen to me or do they just talk at me a great deal like a used car salesperson?' An investor needs to know if the adviser explains ideas and concepts clearly without jargon or too many initials. Do they take time to answer my questions? Do they rush me into making a decision?

"Working with an adviser requires **clear expectations** about outcomes – how much risk for return the investor is willing to trade – the investment approach that the adviser will use on the investor's behalf, and just as importantly, clear expectations about how the relationship will work. Items like how often the adviser and investor will meet, how the investor can reach the adviser with questions, scope of services the adviser is offering and so forth. Some advisers will give advice about non-investment matters and many won't. For example, will the adviser give advice on an investor's 401(k) plan, do retirement planning with a client, or advice on buying a rental property? The investor needs to know what to expect from her adviser in all aspects.

"We've talked about costs a little so far, but if the investor is going to use an adviser, there needs to be a clear understanding of what to expect in terms of costs. After all, every dollar the investor pays to manage her investments is a dollar out of her pocket.

"Finally, I believe no one should hire an adviser that is not a **fiduciary**, which I will explain. I don't think we've talked about the dual standard that exists in the financial industry, have we?"

Donna and Paul shook their heads no and I continued. "I didn't think so. A fiduciary is someone that is legally required to act in the client's best interests, avoid conflicts of interest and operate with complete fee transparency. A lawyer or CPA are fiduciaries and you would think that the investment advisers are fiduciaries, but most are not. I'll say that again: most financial advisers are not fiduciaries. They are not required to act in the investor's best interest. Most advisers are only required to make an initial recommendation to a client to buy a security or product that that is 'suitable' for them. That's pretty vague to me. What is 'suitable' anyway?

"Strange as it may seem, most financial advisers operate under this ambiguous suitability standard and to me that makes no sense. The fiduciary standard means an adviser works for you, in your best interests and with your goals in mind at all times. An adviser that falls under the suitability standard works for his or her employer and in their own best interests plain and simple."

I paused to let that last point sink in. Donna had a pained expression on her face and Paul looked surprised. Paul spoke first.

"I've never really had that explained to me before. Kind of scary, isn't it. I thought our investment adviser was working for us. He told us that if we made money, he made money and made it sound like he was on our side. You're saying he's not? Donna, what do you think of Tim, our current adviser?"

She sat back in her chair and offered, "He seems like a good guy, but I always wondered how he could work for his employer and us too. It seemed like a conflict of interest to me. And he was never really clear about how he got paid. I asked once and he really didn't give me an answer. I got a vague comment about fees are shown on our statements or something like that, which didn't really answer the question."

I continued, "We can get into the fiduciary issue a little later if you want, but let's look at the two options to see the pros and cons of each. What do you see as the pros and cons of each?"

Donna said, "Well, the pros of DIY seem to be that it's cheaper and I can't really see any other positives, at least for me. The cons are that DIY will take more time on our part and I definitely think we can use the support to stay on track and not get distracted. Paul?"

"We could definitely do it ourselves since if we follow the asset class approach, there's not much math required and Donna can do that. But I'm not sure how interested we are in investing. We want good results, but I really don't want to spend my time doing investing chores. I like to take chances on a stock once in a while, but I know that's not what we're talking about here."

"In terms of using someone to help us," Donna added, "I can see where that is more time-efficient, easier and probably more consistent, but I worry about finding a good adviser I can trust. The fiduciary versus suitability idea bothers me. And it's more expensive than if we do it ourselves. Paul?"

Again, Paul continued. "I agree that using an adviser probably costs more, but it will be easier and much more time-efficient for us. Plus, I've been wondering about some other aspects of our finances and I sure would like someone I can trust to ask questions when I have them. And like you Donna, I want to make sure we have someone I can trust. Someone that's competent and of good character. Steve, I know this puts you in the middle, but how do we choose the right approach for us?"

I smiled and answered, "You two really impress me. You work well together, ask good questions, think things through. I think you could do this yourselves, but I don't know if you want to. Here is what I tell many people who sit where you're sitting. If I may, ask yourself this question and be honest with yourselves. Are you ready to take this on and are you 100% committed? A mentor of mine once said, if you are not 100% committed, you are 0% committed. Think about that as you decide. As I say, I think you can do this, I'm just not sure you want to do it yourself given everything I know about you and how you like to spend your time.

"So think about it and let me know if you have any questions on the DIY vs. DFY approach. We have a self-scoring questionnaire on our website (www.finpath.com/money-matters) that you can take that might help you decide the best approach for you too. Both can work as long as you follow a good investment approach and are committed to the three P's. Okay, let's look at three sample portfolios for three different types of clients."

## Key Points:

- Investing is simple, but not easy:
  - » Simple because there are a small number of principles that determine investment success.
  - » Not easy because:
    - o Investing involves uncertainty most people are uncomfortable with;
    - o Investors can be distracted by noise in financial markets;
    - o The financial industry is set up to separate an investor from her money under the false cloak of providing service.

- Two approaches: DIY or Done for You; both can work
  - » DIY requires: time, interest, minimal math, discipline, emotional maturity
  - » Done for You requires: a trusted adviser, good communications, clear expectations, understanding costs, and the fiduciary relationship
- Fiduciary: legally required to put the client's interest first
- Poor alternative: advisers who recommend "suitable" investments
- Most advisers are NOT fiduciaries.

# Examples of Asset Class Portfolios

CHAPTER 9

"Before I share these with you," I cautioned as I pulled out three sets of simple reports, "Keep in mind that each of these are for investors in different situations."

I looked intently at Donna and Paul and they nodded so I continued, "The reason I stress this is because I don't want you running off thinking 'Steve thinks a 50/50 portfolio is what everyone needs.' Which could not be further from the truth. Each portfolio fits an investor with specific circumstances, goals, time horizons, risk and loss tolerances, etc. There is something like 270 different model portfolios so these are just a small sample. With that as the caution, let me show you three portfolios with specific investment vehicles included.

**The first portfolio is Jane's**. She is single, early in her career, makes a good living in the tech area, is a real striver and she has financial freedom at age 50 as a primary goal. Let me point out a few items on this report. I circled these items:

- Overall asset allocation:    80% stocks/20% fixed income
- Worst one year return :    -39.51% (2008-2009)
- Best one year return:    +55.25% (2009-2010)
- 10 year average annual return:    8.5%
- Primary holdings:

  | | | |
  |---|---|---|
  | » | U.S. small value stocks | 15% |
  | » | U. S. large value stocks | 15% |
  | » | Large non-U.S. stocks | 15% |
  | » | U.S. gov't Bonds | 15% |
  | » | U.S. small cap growth stocks | 7% |
  | » | Non-U.S. bonds | 5% |
  | » | Emerging market stocks | 5% |
  | » | Non-U.S. small cap stocks | 5% |

Disclaimer: Past performance is not a guarantee of future experience. Investment returns will differ from the information shown here.

I said, "You'll notice that the percentages don't add up to 100% because there are other investments in this portfolio, some with smaller percentages, but this gives you a good idea of what Jane's portfolio looks like. In fact, Jane has a total of 12 holdings including stocks in commercial real estate and natural resources companies. Any questions on this example?"

Paul was the first to jump in. "Yeah, I have a couple comments and a question. First, when I look at the worst one-year loss, I'm pretty uncomfortable. A loss like that would hurt. On the other hand, I like the best one-year return! The ten-year average annual return is a little less than I expected though. Is that normal?"

Nodding my approval, I said, "Remember that the 2007-2009 market correction was the worst we've experienced in our lifetime. I think the only worse one on record was the correction in 1929 that lead to the Great Depression. And remember that asset class investing does not prevent a portfolio from losing money or even cratering from an event like that. It's interesting to see the bounce back in 2009-2010 though, isn't it? It gives you an idea of how volatile investment markets can be.

"In answer to your other question, these results are not a guarantee of what might happen in the future. You know the old warning: past results are not a prediction of future performance. Investment results can and do vary from what happened in the past. Donna?"

"Well, I'm surprised at how few investments there are for this person. You said she has a total of 12. I know we have at least twice or three times that number in all of our accounts, right Paul? I like the simplicity of this portfolio. Does this include this person's 401(k) plan too?"

I answered, "Yes, most people are amazed at how simple a diversified asset class portfolio can be. Yet, these 12 ETFs and mutual funds hold over 5,000 different publicly traded companies. And, yes, this does include Jane's 401(k) plan holdings. Her company's plan includes a couple of good index funds that we use for large U.S. companies and large non-U.S. stocks, which is typical. We sort of fill in around what she has in her 401(k) plan to create a diversified portfolio. Remember when I told you that investing is simple, but not easy? This is a good example of the simple part of that idea at work.

I pulled out the second report and slid copies across to Donna and Paul. "Let me show you a second asset class portfolio for a couple who are a little like you. **Mac and Mary** are in their 50's, both work, their kids are little older than yours, and like a lot of us, want to retire someday. They came to us a little late in their life so they're trying to catch up on their investing, but they don't want them to take on too much risk either. Let me point out a few items on their report too. I circled these items:

- Overall asset allocation:     60% stocks/40% fixed income
- Worst one year return :     -30.98% (2008-2009)
- Best one year return:     +42.20% (2009-2010)
- 10 year average annual return:     7.3%
- Primary holdings:
  - » U.S. gov't Bonds     30%
  - » Large non-U.S. stocks     15%
  - » U.S. small value stocks     11%
  - » U. S. large value stocks     6%
  - » Natural resources     5%
  - » REITs     5%
  - » Non-U.S. bonds     5%
  - » Emerging market stocks     5%

Disclaimer: Past performance is not a guarantee of future experience. Investment returns will differ from the information shown here.

"Compare this portfolio to Jane's and tell me what you see," I asked. Donna put both reports side-by-side and Paul did the same. Donna answered first. "Same short list of vehicles and I'm beginning to really like the simplicity part of this. The mix is different though. More U.S. government bonds in this one and fewer stocks."

Paul chimed in, "I see the worst one year return is better too. Still a 31% loss must have shaken this client. I see the rebound is less and the return is less too."

Pleased with what Paul and Donna were noticing, I nodded and said. "Very good, you two. You're seeing the differences between the portfolios of these two clients in very different circumstances. What do you think accounts for this difference?"

Donna looked at me and stated, "Well, it's pretty obvious, isn't it? The asset classes you're using are the same so it's how the money is divided between them, right?"

"Absolutely," I said. "Remember that *the real driver of a portfolio is its asset allocation and not the underlying vehicles or when they were purchased or sold*. You can see that's pretty much true in spades in these two cases. Keep that in mind.

"Mac and Mary have more traditional 401(k) plan options that are not as good as Jane's. We chose the best investment options that are available for them, but they are not passive index funds. Still, most of the difference in these two portfolios comes from how much each client has in each bucket and not the small differences in the underlying vehicles. We invest in an imperfect world and do the best we can with what we have to work with."

"Okay, ready for the third example," I said as I slid another report towards Donna and Paul. "Here is the third portfolio for you to look at. It's for **Diane and Dave** who are getting close to being totally retired in the next year or so, Diane retired last year and Dave will retire next year, I think. He waffles on that detail, much to Diane's displeasure. Their kids are all grown and have families of their own so Diane and Dave are about to start a different kind of life and need a different kind of portfolio now. We call it a 'distribution portfolio' because in a few years, they will be taking money out of their IRAs after they've spent all those years putting money in. Here, let me point out a few facts on their report. I circled these items:

- Overall asset allocation:          50% stocks/50% fixed income
- Worst one year return :          -26.12% (2008-2009)
- Best one year return:          +36.03% (2009-2010)
- 10 year average annual return:          5.8%
- Primary holdings:
  - » U.S. govt Bonds          35%
  - » TIPS bonds          10%
  - » U.S. small value stocks          10%
  - » Large non-U.S. stocks          10%
  - » U. S. large value stocks          6%
  - » REITs          5%
  - » Non-U.S. bonds          5%
  - » U.S. small cap growth stocks          5%

Disclaimer: Past performance is not a guarantee of future experience. Investment returns will differ from the information shown here.

"Thoughts or comments," I asked.

Paul was looking at the three portfolios and started first. "I can really see the relationship between the overall asset allocation and the losses and returns with these three portfolios. This couple has taken much of the loss possibility out of their portfolio, but at the expense of less return. Can they afford that?"

I nodded approvingly, "The short answer is 'yes' because they planned for it. The real question for Diane and Dave was what amount of loss could they stand and still sleep well at night? Remember, they're about to retire so their mindset is very different than someone who is still working and bringing in a paycheck. Diane was very clear that she would trade-off trips and gifts to the grandkids for more peace of mind."

Donna interjected, "I see that something called TIPS are a bigger part of their portfolio than all the others. What is that and why a larger part?"

"Sharp eyes there Donna," I said. **"The two biggest threats to retirement happiness are poor health and inflation.** TIPS are a special type of U.S. bond and one part of our 'insurance plan' against inflation. Investors who follow the asset class investing model may also use natural resources and commodities to guard against the pain of inflation, especially retiring clients.

"Remember, asset class investors don't change the mutual funds or ETFs they use, but they do change how much goes into each of them depending on their situation. **That's one of the benefits of asset class investing; investors don't waste time researching, choosing and monitoring individual mutual funds, ETFs or stocks, and efficiently use all of their time choosing the right mix of asset classes and rebalancing only when necessary.** Most investors and advisers do it the other way around." I grinned at them both. "Sorry, I didn't mean to throw stones at some investors or my adviser brethren."

Donna smiled and Paul nodded. By now they seemed to understand that I was going to wave the asset class investing flag often and vigorously. Pointing at the three sample reports I asked, "Any other questions or comments about these portfolios?

Paul asked, "You mentioned that this about-to-retire couple will be taking money out of their portfolio soon, right? How does someone handle that?"

I replied, "There are several ways to take money out of a portfolio, but it's a different conversation than we're having right now. I would be happy to talk about that with you if you want, but another time, okay Paul?" He nodded and made a note of this point.

Donna was listening and shuffled the three reports in front of her. She offered, "This really helps me to see how to put an asset class portfolio to work, so thanks. I know the devil is in the details, but try as I might to be confused, this all seems pretty clear to me. I actually understand how to build an asset class portfolio. Do I need to know what all these numbers mean on the reports? Like what's duration, oh, and I see average expense ratio? That number is really low. That can't be right, can it?

I was happy to answer both of those questions and continued, "I know there are a lot of numbers on these reports and those are mostly for investors who are really into investing. Probably not something we need to cover right now. But trust me when I say that you are in the 90th or 95th percentile of investors with what you already know now. If you wanted to learn more about concepts like duration, it's not that complicated and probably useful, but are you really interested right now?" Donna shook her head no. "As to the expense number, yes, the .21% average expense number for this portfolio is a really low number compared to what the average mutual fund portfolio looks like. This one for Dave and Diane is an actual number because just about all of their money is invested in their IRAs. Dave is a contractor at his old company and Diane retired last year so this is actually how they are invested.

"Keep in mind that the average mutual fund expense ratio is approximately 1.2% of the total value. As we discussed a little earlier, add in turnover costs and the total cost of a typical market timing mutual fund is 2% or 3% or higher. This is money that comes directly out of the investor's pocket. For Dave and Diane, their total cost is about .3% including turnover costs."

Paul replied, "Real money to them and to us, now that I think about it. Okay, I'm glad we looked at these portfolios too. Donna, you okay if we push ahead?" She nodded.

"Thanks for leading us along, Paul," I said. "I want to spend a few minutes discussing the downside of asset class investing and then we'll wrap up with a section I like to call the challenges of investing success." Paul and Donna looked a little surprised and I was pleased to have confronted their assumptions a little bit.

## Key Points:

- Sample portfolios are representative only and each investor needs a portfolio designed for them.

- Past portfolio performance is not a prediction for future experience.

- A simpler asset class portfolio without many holdings can be efficient and effective:

  » An investor can create an effective and efficient portfolio with as few as 10-12 holdings.

- The major difference between portfolios is how investor's money is divided among asset classes and NOT in differences in underlying investment vehicles.

- Asset class investing does not prevent losses from time to time.

- A retirement portfolio is different because the investor must plan for taking money out.

- Asset class portfolios are much less expensive to operate than the average investor's portfolio; additional costs in most portfolios go to the financial industry. With an asset class portfolio, savings go to the investor.

## Notes:

To signal we were starting a new chapter in the discussion, I sorted the sample portfolios we had been reviewing into a stack, set it aside

# Downsides of Strategic Asset Class Investing

and pulled out a clean pad of paper. "You looked a little surprised a moment ago when I said we're going to touch on the downsides of asset class investing. Before we take another break, I thought it would be useful for us to be honest about the shortcomings of asset class investing." I smiled and continued, "I have given you enough of the benefits so it seems fair to give you the other side, don't you think?"

Donna and Paul nodded their assent so I continued by writing these five words and phrases on the paper in front of us so we could all see them:

*Responsibility belongs to investor*

*Boring*

*Underperformance is expected*

*Down times*

*Simple but not easy*

"Can you see that?" I asked. Donna and Paul leaned in, nodded and I continued, "It may not seem like a downside, but *in asset class investing, the investor is responsible* for the success or failure of their investments. The advantage of using a traditional broker is that the investor can blame him or her. Asset class investing means the investor must 'own' the results. The investor gets the credit and the blame if it doesn't work and here's why.

"Even if an investor uses an adviser to help her create and monitor an asset class portfolio, the investor makes all the decisions. The adviser's role is to present relevant information, have enough research at hand to make it simpler and easier for the investor, answer questions, and help the investor stay on track, but the investor is in charge. Because asset class investing uses simple principles that allow the investor total understanding of the approach, once the investor decides to go this way, there is nowhere to hide. The investor can't blame the adviser for making poor timing choices or choosing bad investments. It's all on the investor."

Paul sat back and said, "I can see how that might be a negative for some people. My friend Martin likes to blame his investment adviser when a stock he owns drops off the table. He told me recently that he lost of bunch of money on a tech company because the adviser recommended it and the stock tanked."

"Right," I said. "Asset class investing is **not** for people who want to play the victim. It's for investors who are willing to take responsibility for their money. You might be surprised by how many people we talk to who are not ready to do that. Let me ask you a question: What would it feel like to own your investment future?"

Donna murmured, "A little scary, but good too. Powerful maybe." She looked at Paul and he nodded in agreement.

"Good, you get it then," I said. "*The second disadvantage to asset class investing is that it's boring.* Like watching grass grow or paint dry. We've touched on this before and I want to remind you because too many investors want excitement from their investments and asset class investing is not that. Many months the investor will do nothing. When there is media frenzy around the stock markets, even when there is really nothing going on, the asset class investor will usually be doing nothing. Remember the three 'P's" of investing success? Which one did I say is the most important?"

Paul grinned and said, "Patience."

I went on, "I hope I'm not being too repetitive here, but in our instant gratification, over-stimulated, screen-dominated world, asset class investing is boring. I like to tell people that if you want excitement, go to a casino. Asset class investing is like tending a garden. "

Donna smiled and said, "Yes, it's good to recognize some of the downsides to investing this way. The first couple of items you mentioned are mostly about behavior. What about something technical?"

"Excellent point, Donna." I knew she liked specifics and facts and I was prepared to share them. "Remember when I told you about how often one asset class leads the list of best performers over the last 20 years?" She nodded. "How often do you think an asset class was at the **bottom** of the list, that is, had the worst return?" I paused, and then continued. "Cash has been the lowest returning asset class six out of 20 years, but the worst performing asset class changes from year to year. For example, in six of those 20 years, non-U.S. stocks were at the bottom of the heap. Of course, in another five of those years, non-U.S. stocks were also at the **top** of the list. Over time, non-U.S. stocks perform just fine as you know, but there are many years when they are up and many years when they are down. This is a core principle of asset class investing that I'll mention here. Have you heard of the statistical idea of 'regression to the mean'? Think of the word 'average' as a synonym for 'mean' to make this simpler."

Donna said, "Sure, regression occurs because if something is a long way below its average the first time it's measured, it will probably be closer to the average the second time it's measured. On the other hand, if it was way above its average the first time, it will tend to be closer to the average on the second measurement."

"Yes," I agreed. "Here is an easy way to picture it," and I drew it like this:

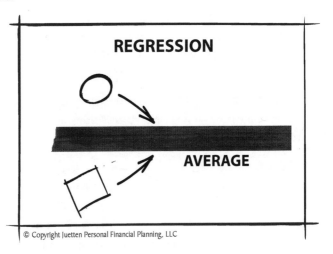

"By the way, in none of the last 20 years was a diversified portfolio at the top or bottom of the list. It couldn't be because a diversified portfolio will always hold asset-class winners and losers so the mix of the portfolio will always be *above* the worst performing asset class and *below* the best performing asset class. Let me draw it for you."

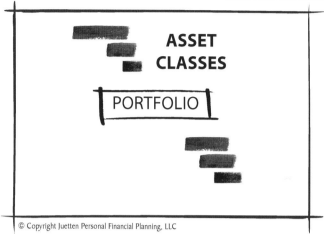

"The point is that in any year, at least one asset class will always underperform other asset classes and the portfolio itself. The tendency for the uninformed investor is to say 'the abc asset class is doing poorly and the xyz asset class is doing great so let's just move all our money to that one.' Can you see the fallacy of that kind of logic?"

Paul nodded and affirmed, "Sure, I can see how that would be easy to do. You look at the abc asset class compared to the xyz one and who wouldn't be tempted to sell abc and buy xyz? But that's exactly backwards, isn't it. When abc is down, an investor should be buying it, right?"

I answered, "Maybe, but as long as both abc and xyz are within the range the investor has for them, the smart thing to do might be nothing. As we talked about during the rebalancing discussion, as long as the asset class is within its range, the investor does nothing. But it's difficult to look at an underperforming asset class and do nothing.

"Accepting that there will always be an asset class or two or three that are underperforming relative to other asset classes is related to the second item we just talked about. If you want to brag about all your winners, asset class investing is not for you. Let's talk about the fourth negative some people see in asset class investing."

I continued, "Remember how when I first drew the risk and return diagram and said that everyone wants to be in the upper left corner where there is no risk and high return?" They both nodded. "And we know that's not possible, right?" Again nods from Donna and Paul. **"There will be down years with an asset class portfolio.** This investing approach does not avoid losses. I know we're talked about 2008, but even in less dramatic years, an asset class portfolio may have a loss. Between 1995 and 2015, it happened three times: in 2001, 2008, and 2015 a diversified portfolio lost money. And it will happen again, I just don't know when. If I did, we could all be billionaires. Some critics point to these down years and use it as evidence that asset class investing doesn't work. I don't believe any investor can claim they have never lost money. Some certainly imply it, but none that I know of actually avoid losses every year, unless they invest only in cash.

"Another adviser once said that monitoring your investments is like watching a girl walk up a hill using a yo-yo; you need to focus on the girl and her steady progress up the hill and not look at the yo-yo." I pulled out a picture and put in on the table.

Paul, engaged as ever, said, "I like that image. I'll remember that one and tell Charles back at the office."

Continuing, I said, "The last downside of asset class investing is one we've talked about before also: it's simple, but not easy to stick with. It's our human nature, I guess. We'll talk more about this after we take a break and go through the challenges of successful investing. What behaviors do you see that make it hard to stick with asset class investing?"

Donna was quick to answer with, "There's the bright shiny object disease where we see something that's new and different and we want that. There's the fact that we're all used to instant gratification and patience is not easy."

Paul nodded in agreement with his wife and added, "And let's face it, we're all greedy and like to keep up with our friends and co-workers. Oh, and don't forget all the noise in the investment world we've talked about. I can't get over how many magazines tout the next great thing or how to beat the market in the new year. And I know what you mean about the 24-7 investment channels. That Cramer guy is crazy. All the noise makes it hard to stick with a passive approach that doesn't have much activity."

I was pleased and could see that they were getting the message loud and clear. "It's really not easy to sit and do nothing most of the time if an investor is used to activity, is it? I saw this cartoon once with two buzzards sitting in a tree. One turns to the other and says, 'The heck with waiting; let's go kill something.' So that's the fifth downside reason to asset class investing. It's simple, but not easy to stick with.

"Let's summarize shall we? Paul, can you start us off?"

He pulled the pad where I had written the five key phrases and words toward him and said, "I think we have them here pretty simply. Asset class investing makes the investor responsible. There is no investment adviser to blame and no 'black box' investing approach to take the fall. Because it's simple to understand, failure must come from the investor.

"Second, it is boring. I can see that. I'm happy to be boring with our investments though. I don't mind having excitement in other parts of my life so this is not really a downside for me, but I can see how some people get addicted to the adrenalin of market timing. Not for me.

"A third problem," he said, pointing at the list, "Is that some would say some asset classes will underperform the others every year. Like you said, a good portfolio will have some above the line and some below the line. An investor has to believe in the math or not.

"The fourth disadvantage is that asset class investing doesn't avoid losses, does it? You said that there were three years in the last twenty in which a diversified asset class portfolio lost money and the investor needs to be prepared for that.

"Finally," Paul said while making a note, "The last downside is one we've talked a lot about. Like you say, good investing is simple because there are only a few basic principles, but it isn't easy to stick with it. There's noise, distractions, bright shiny objects, the media all trying to break an investor's commitment to do things right. I had an old boss who used to say that the secret to success in any business area is not just doing the right things, but doing things right. It seems to apply to investing too. Donna, did I miss anything?"

Donna seemed pleased with Paul and looked at him. "No, I think you did a nice job with that, honey. I'm glad you seem to be getting this too. I want us to be together on the way we invest our money and because this is simple," she looked at me when she said this, "we can both understand it and support each other. No, I think we understand the downsides as you call them, Steve. Although those don't worry me much."

Paul looked down at the note he made on the list and asked, "One thing I've wondered about. It seems like the investment world is changing all the time. How confident are you that asset class investing will work in the future?"

I looked at them both and spoke, "First, nice job on the summary both of you. Well done and as I said, you know more now about investing than just about anyone you'll meet. To your question Paul, I'm very confident that asset class investing will continue to work whatever happens in the future. I believe that because its basic principles are so solid – risk and return are related, the future is unknowable, markets are efficient, invest in a variety of securities that are separate in the way they act, buy the whole forest and don't try to pick individual trees and rebalance when the portfolio gets out of alignment.

"That's pretty much the whole asset class investing owner's manual right there. Of course, it's not easy because human nature doesn't seem to change either – we're driven by fear and greed most of the time and there are some other behaviors we have as humans that work against us too. But, yes, I believe the basic ideas of asset class investing have stood the test of time and will continue to do the same.

"And keep in mind that as new developments occur in the financial world, we can take the best and leave the rest. Like ETFs, which only came about in the 1990's. We use them now instead of mutual funds, but we use them based on the same principles.

"Okay, who's ready for another break? We have one more part to our discussion today and then we can figure out where you want to go from here." I stood up as Donna and Paul did as well. I was anxious to cover the last part of our agenda and as long as Donna and Paul were still interested and engaged, it would be a good conversation until the end.

## Key Points:

Five "downsides" of strategic asset class investing:

- Investor is responsible; no one to blame
  - » Good news: investor owns her/his future
- Boring
  - » Like watching grass grow
  - » Many times investor doing nothing, even when there is media frenzy
- Some asset classes will underperform:
  - » One will be at top each year and one will be at bottom; portfolio is in between
  - » It's random which asset class will be at top and which at the bottom
- Asset class investing does not avoid losses.
  - » Diversified portfolio lost money in 2001, 2008, and 2015
- Asset class investing is simple, but not easy.

# PART 3

# CHALLENGES TO INVESTING
# SUCCESS

# Living With Uncertainty

As we gathered again after the short break, I was a little worried about this next part of the discussion with Paul and Donna. They seemed to be in a good mood, had gained a great deal of knowledge about investing in general and strategic asset class investing specifically and I could sense their confidence growing. We were about to test that.

"All set and ready to dive in again?" I asked. They nodded and I continued. "We've covered a lot of ground in our discussions so far and you've been patient with me and participated fully. I appreciate that." They smiled. "However, for the last part of our chat today, I want to talk about the challenges an investor faces if she or he wants to be a successful investor.

"You've heard me say that successful investing is simple, but not easy. Now we're going to talk more about the reasons that it's not easy. Some of the reasons we've touched on during our earlier talks and some of this will be new, but I want you to fully understand the environment individual investors are in when they decide to start investing so you can be prepared. It's a little like growing a garden on the edge of the woods.

"The gardener is committed to protecting her garden against weeds, pests, animals, and the weather.

She has to remember to fertilize and water the garden and protect it as best she can. Some events she can't do anything about either. A high wind storm, hail, freezing temperatures, too much rain and other natural elements are against her and her garden. But in order to have a successful garden that bears fruit, vegetables and lovely flowers in time, that's what is required.

I looked evenly at Paul and Donna and said, "This may be disturbing to you on some level because much of what I'm going to tell you is kept from the public's view. It's a little sinister when we pull back the curtain on some parts of the financial industry and many investors prefer to be kept in the dark." Donna and Paul shifted uneasily in their chairs and I could almost hear low organ music playing in the background (da da da dum).

"There are actions you can take to protect your investments against the challenges and we'll touch on those too, of course. And you're not totally alone out there either. Think of this as the reality test for being an investor. I wouldn't be doing my job as a fiduciary if I didn't prepare you and any investor for the realities of the job. Ready?"

Donna and Paul looked uncomfortable, but nodded silently for me to continue. I took their silence as assent and said, "This topic got started when I was very early in my career as a financial adviser. Let me tell you the short story.

"A nice young woman and her husband came to me to help her invest a sudden windfall she received when her grandfather passed away and left her a lump sum of money. The windfall was not enough to change their lives, but enough that if they took care of it they could live a good life secure in the knowledge that they had financial resources at an early age that most of us will never have in our lifetime. We call this situation 'sudden money.' Like what happens when someone wins a lottery or someone's start-up company gets bought and her stock options become worth millions.

"When I started working with this woman and her husband, we brainstormed a list of the challenges they faced as new investors. Here is what we came up with and I've used this as an outline with new investors ever since. It's a pretty good list." I wrote these words on the pad of paper in front of us:

Uncertainty

High cost

Wall Street & media

Human nature

Donna and Paul leaned forward to see the list as I continued, "The first challenge is that investing has an essential element of uncertainty that can't be avoided because, as you've heard me say countless times, the future is unknowable. Some people are better dealing with uncertainty than others. But uncertainty is a fact of investing life and an investor has to find the right way to deal with it so she can sleep at night and still make progress towards her goals.

"Questions about what the future will look like frame investment decisions. There are big issues that we can't know the answers to like what the rate of inflation will be, how long will you live, what will happen with Social Security, what taxes will look like and how will my health be over the years.

"And in this environment of uncertainty investors have to make decisions about their capital. It's not easy and I don't want to gloss over this challenge. At its core, the answer to the uncertainty question is having the right investing mindset. Do you believe in the long-term success of the free enterprise system and therefore see the world as generally abundant? Or are you fatalistic or pessimistic, and expect the worst to happen and therefore have a 'scarcity' mindset?"

Donna and Paul looked at me and then at each other and nodded like they got the point I was trying to make. "How do you feel about this part of investing?" I asked them.

Donna started, "I understand your point about living with uncertainty. I can see how the way we deal with this is part of our investing decision process. But it changes, doesn't it? Like with the risk tolerance questionnaires we've completed before?"

I nodded in agreement. "You're right about risk tolerance changing. It seems to change with investors depending on what's going on in their lives and what's going on with the investment markets at the moment. I think of an investor's ability to deal with uncertainty as similar to risk tolerance, but more core to the person's character. For example, some people seem able to charge ahead into the unknown like a new job, new experiences and even trying new food without any problem. Other people are more cautious and want less change and less uncertainty.

"It really goes back to my first SmartMoney Rule™: Have a positive mindset."

Paul interjected, "I know what you mean about some people just seem so positive that things are going to work out and are willing to take chances and others are timid and more fearful. I see that at work all the time. "

"Okay," I said. "You get the point that the first challenge of investing is dealing with uncertainty. Because the future is unknowable, investing requires accepting uncertainty. There is no way around it."

## Key Points:

- First investment challenge: uncertainty
- Successful investing requires accepting uncertainty.
- Best approach to uncertainty: positive mindset

## Notes:

CHAPTER
12

# High Cost

I began again. "The second challenge the successful investor has to face and deal with is the high cost of investing. We've talked about it off and on today and some last week. We'll dive into this topic in depth now. But why is understanding investment costs so important?"

Paul jumped in and said, "Because costs cut down our return. Every dollar we pay for investing our money comes out of our return, right?"

Donna and I both nodded. I said, "You got it. A dollar out of your pocket is a dollar less in return today **and** tomorrow because that dollar used for expenses doesn't have a chance to compound with earnings or interest. That's the insidious part of an investment expense. It reduces your return today and forever." Paul and Donna nodded agreement once more so I continued. "First, the financial industry makes it extremely hard for the investor to find out the true cost of investing. That's one of the reason I am a fiduciary to my clients. I believe in fee transparency, but many in the industry don't. It's unfortunate and wrong, in my opinion, but that's the way it is. The best defense an investor has against high fees is to be aware and ask questions.

"If you search the Internet, you'll find lots of

information on the topic of investing fees and it can get confusing so let me see if I can simplify it and summarize the topic for us. Investment costs come from four sources." I wrote this list:

Product costs

Transaction costs

Brokerage costs

Adviser fees

Donna and Paul leaned forward to look at the list. I charged forward, "**Product fees** are the cost of a owning a mutual fund, ETF or insurance product like an annuity. If you buy an individual stock or bond, there is no product fee, but most of us use these other products. Some advisers invest in stocks and they make their money in another way that we'll talk about next, but for now, let's cover the cost of mutual funds and ETFs.

"Mutual funds and ETFs have published fees that an investor can look up and then hidden fees that are harder to determine. The most obvious fee is a fund's or ETF's **expense ratio.** This is the annual fee that a fund or ETF charges their shareholders. It's a percentage of assets including management fees, research fees, administrative fees, operating costs and all other costs for the fund. It even includes marketing costs, called '12b-1' fees, which makes no sense but is legal.

"Morningstar, a big independent financial information company, estimates that the average mutual fund expense ratio is 1.2% of the amount invested in a fund. An average ETF expense ratio is about

.43% according to some experts. Remember, the expense ratio is just one part of the cost of owning a mutual fund or ETF and we'll get to the other expenses in a minute.

"We have to be careful when we use averages when talking about mutual funds and ETFs. The fees vary by the kind of investments they make. An actively managed mutual fund that specializes in emerging market stocks could have an expense ratio that is double the average. A passive U.S. stock ETF might have an expense ratio that is .10%.

"Put that in dollars and cents for me, will you Steve," asked Paul.

"Sure. If an investor owns $100,000 of a mutual fund with an expense ratio of 1.2%, she pays $1,200 a year. If the same investor owns a passive ETF that invests in the same kinds of stocks with an expense ratio of .43%, she would pay $430 a year. The difference comes out of the investor's pocket."

Donna commented this time, "Not to overreact, but that's real money for a larger portfolio. Makes me concerned about what we've been paying. I looked one time and our investment adviser has us in some pretty high expense ratio funds. We have some ETFs, but mostly mutual funds."

I continued, "Have you ever heard of 'load' and 'no-load' funds?" They looked blankly at me and I continued. "Load funds carry a sales commission and are sold by advisers. No-load funds don't have a sales charge. The funny thing is, every independent study I've seen shows that load funds don't perform better than no-load funds and in fact underperform no-load funds in many cases. There are front-end loads and back-end loads depending on the kind of fund it is. Loads can be 1% or much more – up to 8%! Bottom line: don't buy load mutual funds.

"Now for some of the hidden costs of mutual funds and ETFs," I continued. "Holding cash and being tax-inefficient are also costs for owning some mutual funds and ETFs. There are transaction costs for mutual funds and ETFs, but I want to cover those in the next section so I'll just mention these two here.

"Mutual funds hold cash so they can redeem shares to shareholders who want to sell their shares. It's expensive. Think about it, if you own a mutual fund with a 1.2% expense ratio, you're paying 1.2% for the fund to hold your cash. This is one advantage that an ETF has. They don't hold much cash because ETF shares are bought and sold like a stock.

"The second type of hidden costs is taxes. This applies only to mutual funds an investor holds in their taxable accounts. Basically, a mutual fund incurs capital gains when it buys and sells stocks on behalf of their shareholders. Actively managed mutual funds with high turnover – we'll get to that in a minute – pay high short-term capital gains taxes. Or rather, the investor does. Again, this is an advantage that most ETFs have. They don't run up large capital gain taxes. Morningstar estimates that tax costs can be as high as 1% for an actively managed stock mutual fund."

Paul was scribbling on his pad of paper. "So basically the average mutual fund in a taxable account costs about 2.2% or more and the average ETF costs about .43%, right?

I nodded. "Yup, but that does not include transaction costs that we're going to talk about next. But first, I want to mention the high fees for insurance products. Remember when we first started talking you asked me, Paul, if insurance is an investment like your insurance agent was trying to tell you?" He nodded and I continued, "One of the reasons we don't like insurance as an investment is that insurance products generally carry very high costs, in the neighborhood of 4% or more. There are three basic types of life insurance: term, whole and universal, which is kind of between term and whole life. We also talked about annuities as a kind of insurance product.

"We could do a whole session on life insurance and I won't take the time here, but the challenge of most life insurance products is that it's very hard to understand the costs. Insurance agents are skilled sales people and have gone through extensive training to avoid giving a simple answer to the question 'what does it cost.' Again, it's not that life insurance is a bad idea when used correctly, but the insurance industry does a great job of hiding the true cost when insurance is used an investment. We caution most clients to avoid thinking of life insurance as an investment. Now on to the second type of cost that an investor should know about: **Transaction costs**."

Whenever a security is bought or sold, there are two kinds of costs: the bid and ask spread and a fee for making the trade. Remember we talked about bid/ask spreads when we were discussing ETFs earlier? It's the difference between what the seller is asking for a security and what the buyer is willing to pay. It's usually a few cents for larger ETFs. It's a cost, but usually not a major cost.

"But the second type of transaction cost can be high. Every time a mutual fund or ETF buys and sells a stock or bond on behalf of its shareholders or owners, there is a cost for the transaction and a broker commission. Mutual funds and ETFs deal in huge volume so the cost per transaction is pennies or portions of pennies, but it adds up, especially for market timing funds and ETFs. That brings us to the idea of turnover within a mutual fund or ETF.

"Turnover refers to how often a mutual fund or ETF sells its portfolio holdings. It's kind of like a retail shop. A mutual fund buys a stock or bond for its inventory and then sells it. That's turnover. Care to guess what the average turnover ratio is for actively managed mutual funds? No? Would it surprise you to know that the average mutual fund turns over 85% of its inventory in a year? Some mutual funds have 100% turnover or more in a year. And, as I said earlier, turnover brings with it costs. Turnover costs are not shown in a mutual fund's or ETF's expense ratio either. These fees related to turnover are not easy to find in a prospectus, but the turnover rate itself is easily found online. Some studies show stock mutual funds turnover costs are 1% or more. One study showed them as high as 1.5%. This might be surprising to an investor."

Paul scribbled another note, "So to the 2.2% cost for a typical mutual fund, I can add, what, another 1% or more?" Paul had written these numbers on his pad.

|                   | **MUTUAL FUND** | **ETF** |
|-------------------|-----------------|---------|
| Expense ratio     | 1.2%            | .43     |
| Hidden costs      | 1%              | —       |
| Transaction costs | 1%              | 1%      |
| Total             | 3.2%            | 1.43%   |

I looked at his numbers and nodded. "Yes, that's probably close, but remember that this is for the average actively managed stock mutual fund or ETF. Because it's average, you'll find mutual funds and ETFs that have higher and lower costs than this. For example, if we added up the costs of a passive mutual fund or ETF, the cost would be .5% or in some cases even lower."

Donna was listening and asked, "We talked about this earlier, right? These kinds of costs are one reason that active mutual funds underperform a passive index fund so often?"

I answered, "That's one big reason. Costs do matter when an investor is trying to maximize her investment ROI. Tax inefficiency is another reason and then there is the number of times an active mutual fund manager guesses wrong when they buy and sell a stock or bond. It's expensive when an investor (or his or her adviser) guesses wrong about a security. Buying or selling a security at the wrong time has a cost too." Donna nodded and I continued.

Pointing at the list, I said, "**Brokerage companies** are the next source of high costs for the investor to know about. A brokerage company – sometimes they're called just 'brokerage' or 'brokerage house' – is a big financial institution that puts buyers and sellers together to trade a security. The brokerage company gets paid a commission for managing a trade. For almost 200 years, the only way an investor could buy a stock was through one of these brokerage companies and their agents, the stockbrokers, or brokers for short. Fees were very high and investors had little choice. In 1975, Charles Schwab changed that by starting the first discount brokerage company.

"Now there are full-service brokerage companies and discount brokerage companies. The full-service brokerage companies are names you might know like Merrill Lynch, UBS, Raymond James, Edward Jones, Morgan Stanley Smith Barney and Wells Fargo Advisors. Discount brokerage companies are Scottrade, Charles Schwab, Fidelity, E-Trade and TD Ameritrade.

"We'll talk about these companies more in a few minutes, but for our discussion on costs I wanted you know that most of the brokerage companies have **complicated commission schedules**. Fees vary depending on what the investor is buying, how much and whether the investor places a trade themselves or gets help. It's not simple at all, which isn't fair to the buyer in my opinion. Many investors get duped by this and it's not right. In general, using a broker at one of the full-service brokerage houses to buy and sell is usually the most expensive and doing it yourself online is the least expensive."

Donna asked, "Can you give me an example?"

I thought about it for a minute and answered, "Seems like a simple question, but it's not. Keep in mind that many of the discount brokerage companies have their own mutual funds, like Fidelity and Schwab, and even some of the full service companies now have their own. Trading those are going to be the least expensive and in most cases you won't pay anything to buy and sell those mutual funds at the brokerage company that created them. And some of the brokerage companies have side deals with some of the independent mutual fund companies to offer their funds for free too, so that also complicates it. And some ETFs can be traded for free. Let's try an example anyway.

"Assume you want to buy an ETF from an independent company. For this example, we'll use the iShares ETF that owns the stock of companies outside the U.S. in developed countries (the symbol is EFA). It's one of the largest ETFs and I'm pretty sure you could buy it at any of the brokerage companies. If the investor had a broker at Merrill Lynch buy it for her, the cost would be about $50. If the investor bought it online at Schwab, the cost would be about $9. So you can see there is a big range. As I say, buying and selling securities is complicated when it comes to pricing. It's not like going to Home Depot and asking what does something cost? The answer is 'it depends'. The difference is that at Home Depot they don't charge you a different price if a person helps you find the item or if you check out yourself or use a cashier. Not yet anyway."

Donna smiled and said, "Okay, I can see that there is a big difference in commissions if an investor uses a full-service broker or a discount broker. Anything else we need to know about costs at brokerage companies?"

"Just this," I offered. "As you can probably guess, the brokerage companies don't make money just through commissions. There are so many hidden costs that I can't list them all and I sure don't even know them all. For example, brokers have incentives to sell investors certain high-priced funds and other products instead of cheaper ones. And don't forget, brokerage companies make money when investors buy and sell more often so their brokers have incentives to trade more often too. A guy by the name of Michael Lewis has written several popular books on the shady activities that go on inside brokerage houses. You might want to read one of them. Another author, David Solin, wrote a terrific book titled, *Does Your Broker Owe You Money?* that's a good read too. And there is a terrific book written about 70 years ago titled *Where Are the Customer's Yachts?* You don't need to read these, but if you want to know more about brokerage companies, these are a good place to start.

"In sum, brokerage companies are a necessary evil when it comes to investing. I just want you and all investors to know about them and to use discount brokers when possible, okay?"

Paul and Donna nodded so I continued. "We're covered most of the high cost material and that leaves **adviser fees** as the last item. Remember earlier in our conversation that I mentioned that advisers get paid in one of four ways? To remind you, advisers get paid by commissions for selling products, fees for services, salary and bonuses. Some advisers get a combination of these methods and some are paid in only one way. There are flat-fees and variable fees too. The range of fees paid to an adviser is very large. Some get 8% of the cost for selling insurance and other advisers provide an hourly service that might be only $100. It all depends on the adviser, who she or he works for, the complexity of the service or product the investor wants and the breadth of service that's provided. Mostly, it's buyer beware when an investor engages an adviser.

"And keep in mind that most advisers don't have to tell you what they get paid for a service or product and most won't. They will tell you what the service or product costs, but not what their cut is."

Paul asked, "Why is that a big deal? We bought a car recently and I didn't know or care what the sales person got as a commission?"

Both Paul and Donna asked good questions, which I liked because it meant they were engaged, even at the end of a long day. I said, "Why is that a problem? Good question. Because the investor won't know if the adviser is giving them good advice or just steering them in the direction of what's best for the advisor. Doesn't build much trust in the adviser or the advice he or she is giving, does it? Also, unlike buying a car that might be a $30,000 decision, your portfolio is a million dollar decision. So let me ask you Paul, do you want an adviser who you can fully trust because you know they have your interest in mind first and discloses what he or she gets paid, or do you want an adviser who you aren't sure whose interests they have first?"

Paul nodded, "I see what you mean. I want an adviser that I can trust and that means I need to know she is working for us. I assume the car sales person is working for the dealer and they make commissions, but I choose which car I want not what car they recommend."

"So there you go," I offered. "We've covered the shady and, yes, seedy world of high costs in investing. Remember that the investor can avoid these high costs by being aware of her options and making smart choices. For example, the investor can use no-load and less expensive mutual funds or ETFs, use a discount broker to make trades, insist on knowing how an adviser gets paid and by being aware of the range of fees advisers charge."

Donna added, "And the investor has a huge incentive to keep costs down too. Every dollar an investor pays for investing reduces the return the investor gets. I can see how someone who didn't know about the costs could lose 4% or 5% to these fees with no trouble and not even be aware of it."

## Key Points:

- Second investing challenge: high costs
- Dollars spent in managing investments reduce return now and forever
- Product costs
  - » Expense ratios: average 1.2% for mutual funds and .43% for ETFs
  - » Loads: sales commissions = 1% – 4%; higher for insurance products
  - » Hidden costs = 1% for mutual funds
- Transaction costs
  - » Bid/ask spread

- » Turnover costs = 1% –1.5% for market timing funds
- Brokerage company costs
  - » Complicated commission schedules
  - » Large range of fees
  - » Hidden costs
- Adviser fees
  - » Large range of types and amounts
  - » Types: commissions, fees (flat and variable), salary, incentives, combination
  - » Best practice: ask, understand and agree with adviser
  - » Only fiduciary adviser is committed to full disclosure and transparency on fees.

**Notes:**

# Wall Street and the Media

"Paul, you have a question?"

Paul asked, "I'm confused about something you said when we were talking about brokerage costs a minute ago. You mentioned Wells Fargo Advisors as one on the largest brokerage companies. Isn't Wells Fargo a bank?"

I replied, "Yes and you might be surprised to know that Merrill Lynch is part of Bank of America and Morgan Stanley bought Smith Barney from Citicorp. That leads me nicely – thanks Paul – to the point I was about to make. Brokerage companies are in the business of making money and they will do anything they can to make money from investors. When you work with a brokerage company and their employees – the brokers – you are in dangerous territory. A broker works for their master, the brokerage company, and the broker has every incentive to make money from their customers. Most investors don't realize this and pay the price, literally and figuratively. Remember, a broker does not work for the investor, whereas a financial adviser who is a fiduciary does.

"Brokerage houses are one part of what is generally called 'Wall Street' and Wall Street is the next challenge to investment success an investor faces. 'Wall Street' is a term that refers to all the companies that are in the financial services industry including brokerage houses, mutual fund companies, investment banks and hedge funds. The stock exchanges themselves are part of the financial industry, like the New York Stock Exchange, NASDAQ and even stock exchanges that are not in New York, like the one in Philadelphia. They are all part of this thing we refer to as 'Wall Street.'

"An investor doesn't need to know all the details of Wall Street, but should realize one thing: The companies of Wall Street are not your friends; they are vendors, plain and simple and exist to make their owners money. One unfortunate part of the financial industry is that there are no standard fees they charge customers; fee structures are hard to find and understand. Unlike the car lot we talked about earlier, Wall Street does not post their prices on window stickers. Most of the fees are hidden and the compensation structure of the financial industry encourages conflicts of interest between the company and their customers.

"Speaking of customers, remember that the individual investor is not the only customer on Wall Street. Institutional customers are involved too. These are the elephants in the financial industry like pension plans, insurance companies, commercial trusts, endowment trusts, hedge funds and investment banks. They're out there competing with the individual investor for products and services. It's essential to keep in mind who you're rubbing elbows with when you're in the financial world. It helps the investor to understand how certain parts of the investment world works, for example, that there are multiple fee schedules for different customers.

"And the point I want to remind you of is that few, if any, of the Wall Street companies are fiduciaries for you as the investor. Remember that **a fiduciary is required to act in your best interest.**

with open books on fees and to avoid conflicts of interest with you and to disclose them when they can't be avoided."

Paul jumped in and added, "Yes, the dual standards are really pretty strange. A fiduciary is required to act in an investor's best interest but a stockbroker is not? They just need to do what they decide is suitable for the investor, which seems pretty squishy and vague to me."

I nodded in agreement with Paul because he was right and I was glad he understood this important point. I was almost done with my Wall Street background speech, but wanted to touch on another part of The Street. "You got it Paul. This double standard of care for customers is strange indeed and many investors don't realize it exists. You do so that's reassuring.

"The last part of Wall Street I want to mention is insurance companies," I continued. "We've touched on them a couple of times in our discussion, but I want to bring them up again specifically because they are all around us. I was watching a football game the other day and counted five different insurance ads during the game. As I said, insurance is a good thing when it's used for its primary purpose: to shift the risk of a large loss away from the individual or family. Investing, on the other hand, is meant to grow and protect your wealth. So when your friendly insurance agent tries to get you to buy a product that he or she positions as an investment, ask them to be clear if they're talking about insurance or investing. That will put them on notice that you know the difference.

"The biggest drawbacks of insurance products meant for investing are the high cost and complexity of most of them. One of the most popular investment products sold by insurance companies are annuities. You've heard of them, right?"

Donna shifted in her seat and said, "Yes, but mostly in ads and on TV. Our insurance guy mentioned them a couple of times and touted them as a great way to make sure we have a steady stream of income when we retire. That sounds pretty good, but I haven't looked into them. Should we?"

I replied, "It depends. Annuities are a whole subject unto themselves, which should tell you something. But since you and many other investors are exposed to them, let's take just a few minutes here and go over the basics. If you want to learn more, there is a terrific book by a colleague that I can recommend so you can learn more. If you want to talk to an insurance person about them, I can recommend a couple of companies that we direct clients to when they are interested. Okay with you?"

Paul said, "That's fine. What's the name of the book? I might be interested in learning a little more."

"Sure Paul," I said. "Look up a financial educator by the name of Todd Tressider. He has a free online tutorial on annuities that I recommend and his book is *Variable Annuity Pros and Cons*. Todd is a terrific financial coach and a straight shooter. He's not a financial adviser per se, but knows a lot about financial products and the industry. I highly recommend you check him out on this topic."

"Briefly, an annuity is a financial product sold by an insurance company. The investor puts after-tax money into the annuity and the value grows tax-deferred until the investor takes the money out. Typically, the investor receives payouts for her or his lifetime. That's the stream of income that your agent touts, Donna.

"The big selling point for annuities is the investor can't outlive their income. Social Security retirement income is an annuity in that way too. That's the simple explanation of what an annuity is. From here it gets complicated. I would check out the Tressider book if you are interested in more details. But do remember there are two basic kinds of annuities: fixed and variable. With a fixed annuity, the payout is guaranteed by the insurance company. With a variable annuity, the amount of payout is uncertain.

Paul, the more interested of the two spoke up, "Lifetime stream of income sounds pretty good. But I can do the same thing by saving money in a savings account and taking it out a little at a time when I'm ready, right?"

"Yes, of course," I said. "The advantage of the annuity method is that they offer higher returns with no taxes on the earnings until you take out the money. As you know, you sure don't earn much with a savings account and anything you do earn is taxed at your current income tax rate. The advantages of an annuity are compelling, but as Donna knows and has said, the devil is in the details, right Donna?" She nodded with a smile and I continued.

Paul said, "I get that annuities are complex and can be expensive and I also see some advantages, but I'm not convinced annuities are a good idea for us. Donna, you agree?"

She responded, "I see the attraction of a stream of income, but Steve points out the high cost and complexity and I don't really want to educate myself that much on this right now."

"I agree," I said. "My colleague Todd likes to say that very few annuities are **bought** by educated consumers. Most are **sold** by good sales people. I tend to agree with him. Check out his materials on the subject though. In some circumstances, we do recommend single premium immediate annuities for people. Not often, but it does happen. "

"Let me finish this part by just mentioning again the role that the media plays in investing and why I list it as one of the challenges. It's not an accident that I put Wall Street and the media together in this section of our discussion. As Donna said earlier in our conversation today, hype sells. I can't emphasize enough how good the media is at getting our attention to sell us something and making it seem like it's helpful. Most if not all the TV time spent on investing is worthless. Same thing for the financial magazines. The advertisers in these magazines are mostly financial service companies who are trying to sell you their products and services. Even newspapers are willing accomplices. So watch out for the media when it comes to financial matters. They are in bed with the financial services industry and willing co-conspirators in separating investors from their money. One financial adviser I know calls the financial junk the media spews out 'financial porn.' That gives you an idea of how strongly he objects to it.

"So there you have it. Have we talked enough about Wall Street and the media as a part of the investment landscape so you feel like you know how they affect you?"

Donna answered, "Yes, but one question. I read about the SEC being involved in the financial world sometimes. Aren't they supposed to be watching over Wall Street to make sure everything is legal and the investor is protected? I hear about Bernie Madoff and what's her name, the famous woman who went to jail for insider trading?"

Paul jumped in, "You mean Martha Stewart?"

Donna said, "Yes, that's right. Martha Stewart. What about the SEC and other government departments? Aren't they part of the environment?"

I pondered how to answer this question. "Yes, they are part of the landscape for investors. You can't completely protect yourselves and there are groups that are providing some protection like the SEC. But rather than take a long time to talk about it today, you can find out more about these watch dog agencies on our website (www. finpath.com/money-matters).

## Key Points:

- Third and fourth investment challenges: Wall Street and the media

- The term "Wall Street" includes anyone connected to the financial industry in the U.S. including brokerage companies, insurance companies, mutual funds, investment banks, and the people who work for them.

- Wall Street exists to make money for the companies not the investor.

- The individual investor competes with institutions including pension funds, insurance companies, big trusts and hedge funds.

- Insurance companies sell insurance and investment products, like annuities, which are complex and usually expensive.

- The media are willing co-conspirators to sell products that may not be in an investor's best interest.

- There are government and non-government entities that protect investors, like the SEC, but complete protection against fraud and other wrong-doing in the investment world is not possible.

**Notes:**

# Human Nature

Donna asked, "I know we're about to talk about human nature as the last challenge, right?" I nodded and she continued. "And I've been thinking a little about that. I think this may be the hardest challenge to deal with when it comes to investing." Looking at Paul, she said, "In so many ways, we are our worst enemy when it comes to our investments. Just thinking about all the mistakes we've made in investing, it's pretty discouraging. That's why we go back and forth between thinking we need help and hiring an adviser and then we see that they don't do much and we pay for it and then try to do it ourselves. Like you say, investing may be simple, but sure isn't easy when you throw the human elements into it."

Paul jumped in agreeing with Donna, "And it's not just about our mistakes either. It comes down to time, for me. Like I said early on in our conversations, I'm not sure I want to spend my time doing this. I like to do fun activities with Donna and my friends with my free time and I like my job and it takes time to do it right too. I have to say that I don't really get my kicks doing investing tasks either. I'm not like my friend Charles at work, the one who loves to try to pick the next hot stock. That's not me."

I said, "I get it. And you're right. It's not just the

mental and behavioral mistakes that investors make that holds them back from reaching their investment goals. It takes time and interest in the subject to invest successfully on your own. So let's walk through the last challenge to successful investing a bit more, human nature.

"First, I want to remind you about an ongoing study that I shared with you earlier done by the Dalbar group. If you recall, the study shows that individual investors under perform an unmanaged index – the S&P 500 – by an average of approximately 5% per year. In 2014, the difference was 8%. Why do you think that is?"

Paul guessed, "From our discussions, I know part of the reason is that most individual investors are market timers, right? They're trying to beat the market and make all sorts of mistakes like buying and selling too frequently, letting the media influence them so they follow the herd, actions like that, right?" Donna added, "Or the opposite: not paying attention, not rebalancing when they should or paying really high fees."

"You're both right," I said. "The majority of mistakes that Dalbar noted come from loss aversion and herding. This is the behavior gap that Carl Richards, the adviser I like so much, mentions. Loss aversion leads to panic selling and you know what herding is. I won't go over all the biases we bring to investing, but they include behaviors like confirmation bias – following our preconceived conclusion and finding evidence to support it. Investors tend to be overly optimistic and overestimate their abilities too.

"Sometimes investors are paralyzed by the number of choices they have. CNBC is on sometimes when I'm at the gym and I'm amazed by the amount of information they spew out. A normal person would be overwhelmed by all the information and probably freeze up and do nothing. Or just think of the number of mutual funds and ETFs that are out there. Another bias is that investors prefer stories to data. It's understandable because a great story is much more compelling than a chart or graph by itself. But this bias tends to confuse us. Too often the investor confuses luck with skill.

"One of my favorite biases is what is called a 'recency' bias. We tend to put too much emphasis on events that have happened recently and lose sight of the longer view. This is one reason we urge investors to use the three P's: perspective, persistence and patience.

"To give you example of recency, one study showed that so-called market experts recommended a high concentration of stocks just *after* the Internet bubble peaked. An example of buying high. This same group of experts recommended the lowest concentration of stocks just *after* the lows of the Great Recession in February 2009. An example of selling low. This is recency at work.

Donna added, "I see that in my work and at home too. At work, we tend to think that whatever is going on with sales recently is going to continue and that's not the case. We see short-term ups and downs in sales, but the long-term trend is up. We forget that."

"Exactly," I continued, "We all have blind spots when it comes to our biases. The best way to offset these biases is to be aware of them and factor that in when we think about making an investment decision. We tell investors that a key principle is to know yourself as an investor. That's one of the reasons we spend so much time on the discovery step when we start working with a new client. Yes, it's important for us to know a client, but it's equally important for the client to know themselves. We believe an investor needs to be honest with him or herself and that means taking a hard look at your biases.

"Anyway, moving on," I said. "We've touched on this before and

I want to bring it up front and center now. The question is, how do you want to use your time? We all have the same amount available to us each day. And we all have huge demands on our time every day. Family, fun, exercise, chores that can't be avoided like cleaning, and of course work. It's a regular balancing job we do every day."

Donna broke in, "I know where you're going with this one and I agree. I ask myself this all the time: What is the best, most useful way for me to use my time? There are things I *must do* and things I *like to do* (like spending time with Paul, activities with friends, and when the kids were home, helping them and being involved with their activities). I've told you that being involved in regular investing chores is not high on my list. I know I should pay attention to our investments because it's important, but because I don't like it, I avoid it and then outcomes happen that are disappointing. Like we've said, we either hire someone we don't entirely trust or we try to do it ourselves and end up not doing it well."

Paul added, "I'm with Donna on this, as I've said. When I think of what my hourly rate is at work and apply it to the time I spend doing investing tasks – and not doing them very well – I cringe. But we need to do something to take care of our money. That's why we're here with you, Steve. To see if there is a better way to invest."

Nodding I said, "You're right. Successful investing requires time to do it and interest; if you don't like it, you will avoid it as Donna said. But don't despair just yet; with what we've talked about here, I'm confident you can find the right balance for you.

"One more point to make about human nature and investing and then I want to talk about the differences between men and women when it comes to investing." Paul raised an eyebrow towards me and I knew he would be interested. I continued, "The last human nature challenge to mention is one we've touched on before…investing as competition.

"Meir Statman is a finance professor at Santa Clara University. He likes to use this image: Some investors imagine they are tennis players hitting the ball against the wall. They say to themselves, 'If I do this, that will happen. If I hit the ball this hard with this spin, it will bounce this way off the wall.' Others imagine they are playing a faceless opponent that is equal to them in skill. The reality is that the investor is playing against Pete Sampras or Serena Williams, arguably the greatest tennis players in history. The individual investor has no chance if she or he thinks of investing as competition.

Paul chimed in, "I know. That's how my friends think sometimes. They see investing as a game that they can win and show off their prizes. I admit that sometimes I get sucked into that kind of thinking. I don't think they know the difference between gambling and investing."

I added, "And men are generally more into competition than women are and it's one reason that men are generally worse investors than women. Paul, I know you raised your eyebrow when I mentioned this earlier."

Donna observed, "I think there are more women taking control of the finances in their families than when I first started working. Is that part of it?"

Nodding, I said, "First, let me say that generalities about gender differences are indicators and not absolutes. There are many studies being done about this subject, but there are exceptions to every study and I don't want you think I'm making judgments. I just thought you might find this interesting to discuss for a minute or two.

"A study that Fidelity[6] did a few years ago showed that more women are handling the day-to-day money responsibilities at home than ever before. About one in four women run the finances at home and about one in five make the investment decisions. Many households, probably like yours from what I can see, the financial decisions are made jointly, but someone has to do the day to day tasks, right?" Donna and Paul nodded in agreement. I continued, "Here are some attributes of women investors compared to men investors.

"First, women tend to have a longer term view than men and are more patient. Women generally do more research on investments. They also tend to remain steady under pressure and therefore trade less than men. One study showed that men trade 45% more overall compared to women and we know from our earlier discussion that one outcome of frequent trading is that investors usually sell at market bottoms. In the big market drop in 2007 and 2008, a Vanguard study found that women cashed out 10% less than men.

"And here's a big difference: Men are more overconfident about their investing prowess than women and that leads to mistakes. Women are more likely to admit when they don't know something and will learn about it. Men tend to believe their interpretations of news and facts are correct and believe they can make profitable investing decisions based on their views. We know how well that works."

Paul laughed and said, "Okay, okay. I get it. Men are worse investors than women. I can see where that leads." I responded, "I'm not saying that all men are worse investors than women or that all women are better investors than men. But you can see where the differences are useful to recognize. One way to think about this is that all the

---

6 Fidelity Investments Money FIT Women Study

investment biases that we talked about earlier tend to show up in men more than women. I don't know why, they just do."

Donna joined in on the lightness of this topic and laughed. "I get it that both men and women have biases that get in their way. We women sometimes don't spend enough time on finances and I don't like to see women just give it all over to their husbands or partners either. That seems dangerous too. Like you said, about one in four women are in charge of the household finances and the trend is growing, but we do it jointly, don't we Paul?" "Yes we do" he replied.

I shifted back in my seat and said, "Guess what my friends? We've reached the end of this session. Before we end, are there any other questions or topics we need to touch on? Anything we need to review or cover that we've haven't?

Paul and Donna looked at each other and shook their heads. "Okay," I said, "Let's wrap up then."

## Key Points:

- Human nature may be greatest challenge to investment success.

- Dalbar study shows individual investors under-perform an index by 5%/ year, mostly due to decision biases:

  » Fear of loss leads to panic selling

  » Wanting to do what everyone else is doing

  » Too many choices leads to decision paralysis

  » Placing too much emphasis on what's happened most recently

- Two key questions:

- » How does the investor want to use her/his time?
- » How much interest does the investor have in investing?
- Investing is not a competition. The only way to win is not to compete.
- Men and women are different investors in key ways:
  - » Women are more patient, take the longer view, trade less, do more research, learn more willingly, less over confident in their interpretation of events.
  - » Men trade too much, see investing as a game, are short-term oriented, believe their view of the world is correct and can profit from that knowledge; stubborn.

**Notes:**

# Conclusion: What If?

I looked at Donna and Paul and started to say something sentimental. I had grown fond of them in our short time together. They were good students, nice people and a good couple. Instead though, I asked, "Let me ask you a couple of questions. First, how would you define successful investing?"

Donna and Paul were thoughtful for a minute and Paul started, "Being a successful investor means having a way to invest our money that helps it grow with the amount of short term ups and downs we can live with. We're using the word 'volatility' for that, and the approach we use has to have a high probability of us having enough capital to meet our goals." Donna added, "And to do it in a way that we can stick with over time with the amount of time and effort we choose to give to this activity."

I replied, "I like that. Here are the keys ideas I heard you mention." I wrote on a blank sheet of paper from the pad in front of me.

Grow wealth

Balance short-term volatility
Long-term success

*Fits goals & time horizon*

*Sustainable*

*Efficient*

"Did I get that right?" I asked. Paul and Donna nodded and I continued, "So given this definition, what do you see as the benefits of Strategic Asset Class Investing now that you have a working understanding of what it is and how it works?"

Donna leaned forward, "As we've talked about asset class investing, I can see the benefits to us pretty clearly. It's certainly effective, especially compared to market timing. It's pretty simple to create a portfolio and operate it from what we've discovered. There are no difficult or confusing ideas in this. I like the simple part. Because it's simple, we can understand it even though we're not experts and don't want to be experts. I can see where asset class investing is flexible too. And probably the biggest benefit to us is that it's efficient. Whether we use someone to help us or do it ourselves, asset class investing uses our time well. As you know, that's a big item for Paul and me.

I nodded in appreciation and Paul added, "I agree with Donna on all of those and I like the fact that asset class investing helps us navigate our way through the challenges you listed to successful investing: uncertainty, high costs, Wall Street, the media and ourselves. It seems to me that we want to be smart with our money and find a good way to overcome the ditches and potholes that seem like they are just part of the investing landscape. We can avoid most of them if we're smart in the way we invest."

I nodded again and said, "I agree with everything you've listed. Good job. So let me ask you one last question. What if you could be in control of your investing approach? What if you 100% believed in what you were doing? What if you had confidence in how you were investing? What then?"

Donna looked at Paul and Paul looked back with a wry smile on his face. She answered for them both it seemed. "That would be success."

I laughed and stood up and they did too. They thanked me, we shook hands, and they agreed to be in touch in a week or so to let me know how they would like to proceed. That was okay with me. I knew that whatever they decided, however they chose to proceed, that they would be fine in the end. As far as I was concerned, our discussions were a success.

**Notes:**

# Epilogue: Investing During Retirement

Several months after the conversations with Paul and Donna, the phone rang in my office. "Hello, this is Steve Juetten," I answered. The caller replied, "Hi Steve. This is Bonnie Schultz. My husband Ed and I are friends of Paul and Donna Moore. Ed and Paul used to work together and Donna and I got to be friends through them. Anyway, Ed and I are getting close to retirement and we're not sure how we're going to handle our retirement money. Donna and Paul speak highly of you and suggested we give you a call to set something up."

"Thank you Bonnie for calling me," I said. "I like Donna and Paul a great deal and any friend of theirs is a friend of ours and all that. Do you have a little time right now to tell me about your situation? I know you said that you're close to retirement, but would you please share the rest of the story?"

She continued, "Sure. Well, like I said, we're starting to think about retirement because Ed would like to stop what he's doing in two or three years and maybe work part time and we'd like to be a little closer to our kids and the grandkids. I'm an independent contractor and can work from anywhere, but our overall concern is managing our money when we retire. And we have questions about when to take Social Security and whether we should pay off our house wherever we live. "

"Yes, there are a lot of factors to consider when you retire, aren't there," I answered. Bonnie continued. "We both have 401(k)'s and IRAs and Roth IRAs too. We have some stock from the company Ed works for now and a small brokerage account. Donna told us to check out your website and I see that you suggest using something called the 'three bucket approach in retirement.' I'm not sure how that works."

I was encouraged that she had taken the time to look at our company website and read the section about investing in retirement. I continued, "I'm glad you read that little piece. Basically, the three bucket approach divides your money among three buckets: One holds your annual planned spending, the second contains fixed income investments like CDs and short-term bonds and the last bucket is for stocks. Money flows into bucket one from bucket two each year and periodically, when stocks have had a good year, money goes into bucket two from bucket three. Does that help?" I doodled a picture of the three buckets on my pad of paper.

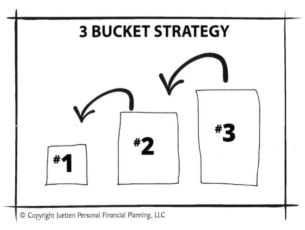

3 BUCKET STRATEGY

#1  #2  #3

© Copyright Juetten Personal Financial Planning, LLC

Bonnie replied, "I understand about the buckets, but how do we choose what goes into each bucket? Do we just choose mutual funds and stocks? That seems like a lot of guessing. I know Donna said you don't believe in trying to pick stocks."

Again encouraged by Bonnie's interest and questions, I answered, "We use the same approach for helping investors at all points in their lives. From starting out to retiring, we use an approach called "Strategic Asset Class Investing' or ACI for short. Basically, ACI uses different asset classes to create an overall portfolio. An asset class is a security that acts differently than other securities. For example, stocks, bonds and cash are different asset classes. We try to put together a portfolio of asset classes that are as different from one another as possible. The idea is that when one asset class is going down, another one is going up.

"Most investors are trying to balance risk and reward and the asset class investing approach allows us to create a portfolio that matches potential risk and return for each investor. Every investor has a different tolerance for short term ups and downs – we call that volatility – and has a different amount of risk they are willing to take to reach their investment goals. Does that help?"

I could hear Bonnie hesitate on the other end. "I think so. I know we are way more scared of the stock market now compared to when we were younger. And speaking of worries, our biggest worry is outliving our money and being a burden on our kids."

I replied, "I understand. There are lots of changes that come with retirement and one of them is a person's mindset. When the investor no longer has a paycheck, it changes the way the investor looks at their nest egg, doesn't it?"

I could almost see Bonnie nodding at the other end. "So let me see if I understand what you're saying. The three buckets hold our annual spending budget, fixed income securities and stocks. The idea is to put different securities into each of them. You call these asset classes, right? And an asset class is a kind of a security that acts differently than other securities. You use this approach for investors no matter what phase of life they're in. Did I get that right?"

I wanted to add one final point so I said, "You got it, Bonnie. Investing when a person is 35 is different than a person who is 55 and different for a person who is 65. But the same basic approach of mixing asset classes to fit the investor is the same for them all.

"Investing in retirement is different in one important way than during the other times in a person's life and you touched on it. During retirement, an investor is taking money out of their accounts that they've spend a life time putting money into with no regular income to replace it. **How much** the retiree takes out is key, of course, as is **when** the money comes out and **what assets are sold**. It's simple, but not easy."

Bonnie responded, "Well, you say it's simple, but I'm not so sure. And what about the other questions we have, like about Social Security and Medicare and our mortgage?"

I answered, "They're all pretty much tied together aren't they? Having confidence in your finances and good health are the building blocks of a happy retirement. After that, the three keys to retirement happiness are:

1. Where you live

2. What you do

3. Who you do it with

"My company created some free tools that might help you and Ed as you think about retirement. One of them is a retirement readiness quiz that you can use to do a self-assessment. You can get that at www.readysetretirequiz.com. I suggest that you take it to see how ready you both are. We also created some retirement planning checklists that will help you go through the important action items as you countdown to retirement.

You can get those at www.retirementchecklists.com. What else can I help you with today Bonnie? I hope I've answered at least some of your questions?

She answered, "You've been a big help, Steve. I can see why Donna and Paul recommended you. And they said you're a fiduciary too, right?"

I answered, "Yes, as you probably know that means I'm legally required to put my clients' interests first and the only people that pay us are our clients. We don't sell products or get commissions. A lot of what passes for retirement planning involves selling people products like complicated and expensive annuities and high cost services."

Bonnie said, "I like that you're a fiduciary for sure. We don't want anyone selling us anything. Okay, you've been great, Steve and I feel a little better. Thank you. Can Ed and I come in to see you and talk more about the three buckets and asset classes and all the other items we've touched on today?"

"Sure," I said. "Let me send you my schedule and you and Ed can pick a convenient time to come to our offices and we'll have a nice chat."

After we exchanged email addresses and said goodbye, I hung up and went back to what I was doing. It seemed like Bonnie and

Ed would be an enjoyable couple to meet. As usual, I was curious to see where the road would take them in their journey into the phase of life called retirement. I knew that they faced a great deal of uncertainty and new adventures in the months ahead. They might be crossing over into the desert and wandering for a while, but with a clear vision of what their Promised Land looks like, I was confident they could get there. I hoped I could help guide them.

# Bibliography and Resources

**Books**

*The Four Pillars of Investing* by William Bernstein

*Common Sense on Mutual Funds* by John Bogle

*Does Your Broker Owe You Money?* by Daniel R. Solin

*Winning the Losers Game* by Charles Ellis

*A Random Walk Down Wall Street* by Burton G. Malkiel

*The Coffeehouse Investor* by Bill Schultheis

*The Only Guide to a Winning Investment Strategy You'll Ever Need* by Larry Swedroe

*The ETF Book* by Richard A. Ferri

*Variable Annuities Pros and Cons* by Todd Tressider

*Why Smart People Make Big Money Mistakes* by Gary Belsky and Thomas Gilovich

*The Behavior Gap* by Carl Richards


**Resources**

Morningstar (www.morningstar.com)

Juetten Personal Financial Planning website (www.finpath.com)

Garrett Planning Network (www.garrettplanningnetwork.com)

Securities and Exchange Commission (www.sec.gov)

Dimensional Fund Advisors (https://us.dimensional.com)

# About Steve Juetten, CFP®

*"People hire me for my head, pay me for my heart, and trust me most when I use both."* – Steve Juetten, CFP®

Since 2002, busy career professionals have trusted CERTIFIED FINANCIAL PLANNER™ practitioner Steve Juetten for personal financial guidance. All are treated to the same simple, respectful and direct counsel that comes from being raised in the Midwest and loving what he does.

Steve helps clients identify where they want to go in their lives, evaluate where they stand now from a financial perspective and help them create and follow the financial steps that guide them to achieve their goals.

He is a fee-only financial adviser and is a fiduciary for his clients. "Fee-only" means that Steve does not sell any products (other than an occasional book he writes!) or take commissions so clients can trust his objective, independent advice and counsel. As a fiduciary, Steve is legally required to put his clients' best interest ahead of his own, avoiding conflicts of interest and operating with fee transparency.

Steve has been a featured expert on Bankrate.com, PBS.com, Forbes.com, MSNMoney.com, FOXBusiness.com, and the *Puget Sound Business Journal.* His clients seem to like what he does to help them. *Seattle Magazine* has named Steve a FIVE STAR WEALTH MANAGER for five years in a row.

Steve is the Managing Member and Principal of Juetten Personal Financial Planning, LLC, a Registered Investment Advisor firm located in Bellevue, Washington (www.finpath.com). He leads a small team of dedicated professionals committed to helping their clients achieve their goals through careful application of a 360° financial planning and investment management system.

If you'd like to schedule a time to talk with Steve or a member of his team, please email him at ditchtheguesswork@finpath.com, or call at 425-373-9393. Groups rave about Steve's engaging workshops and speeches on such topics as the Five Retirement Blunders Even Smart People Make, How to Retire Successfully and Ditch the Guesswork. If you would like to book Steve for your event, please contact him.

# Index

Proof